Preface

THE OPPORTUNITY TO publish a book would have been a great privilege at any time in history, but perhaps especially now. After all, this book could be one of the last ones. What a relief that would be, eh? All those tightly bound conduits of empathy and insight turned to ash and smoke, all of humanity dancing in a ring around the bonfire as we usher in a new era of expression wherein communication takes the form solely of disinterested teenagers prowling the streets, thrusting lavalier mics into the faces of unsuspecting strangers, demanding to know what they're listening to, how much money they earn, how many people they've slept with.

With ravenous glee, tech overlords are seeking to

1

dehumanise art, to saturate us with low-quality writing and audio and video (all under the umbrella of 'content') and before you know it, *At Least It Looks Good From Space* will be sitting on the very last shelf, on the very last stack, down the very back of an Indiana Jones hangar in Fort Knox where they keep one copy of every book ever printed just in case they ever need more kindling.

Seeing as it's such a privilege, then, it seems only right that anyone who gets the chance to publish a book should approach the prospect with a formidable sense of purpose. It seems a crime that so much as a sentence should go by without impressing upon the reader the perceptible weight of intentionality. A cohesive and clearly articulated world view, something like a mission, built upon hard-earned conclusions, which themselves emerge from careful, thoughtful premises.

That's not really my style, unfortunately. Throughout my life, I've found that the things I do by mistake end up making at least as much sense as the things I do on purpose – if not more.

This book does set out to do a few things. It is a collection of essays that explores themes of millennialism, mental illness and masculinity. What it means to be young but not that young, disordered to varying degrees, a man but not that much of a man.

AT LEAST IT LOOKS GOOD FROM SPACE

Carl Kinsella is a writer from Dublin who rarely lasts longer than a year in whichever city he's living in. He writes a weekly social commentary column for *The Journal* called 'Surrealing in the Years', a name he came up with himself. He has twice been nominated in the 'Popular Columnist of the Year' category at the Irish Journalism Awards. He lost both times, but whatever, it's not a big deal. Kinsella writes for the BBC Radio comedy show *Lunchtime with Michael Fry*, and serves as something like a news correspondent on the popular podcast *Catch Up with Louise McSharry*.

At Least It Looks Good From Space is his first book.

A catalogue of modern, millennial and personal catastrophes

AT LEAST IT LOOKS GOOD FROM SPACE

CARL KINSELLA

HACHETTE
BOOKS
IRELAND

First published in Ireland in 2025 by HACHETTE BOOKS IRELAND

1

Cataloguing in Publication Data is available from the British Library.

ISBN 9781399751513

Excerpt from 'Transport authority contacted gardaí over Twitter account after fake 'free Luas' claims went viral' by Cónall Thomas, *The Journal*, 1 September 2021, used with permission.

Typeset in Bembo Book Std by Bookends Publishing Services, Dublin.
Printed and bound in Great Britain by Clays Ltd, Elcograf S.p.A.

Hachette Books Ireland policy is to use papers that are natural, renewable and recyclable products and made from wood grown in sustainable forests. The logging and manufacturing processes are expected to conform to the environmental regulations of the country of origin.

Hachette Books Ireland
8 Castlecourt Centre
Castleknock
Dublin 15, Ireland
email: info@hbgi.ie

Authorised representative in the EEA

A division of Hachette UK Ltd
Carmelite House, 50 Victoria Embankment, London EC4Y 0DZ

www.hachettebooksireland.ie

Dedicated to the memory of Willie and May Connell

Contents

Threaded through these reflections is the omnipresence of the internet and the influence of online platforms that now loom over the modern digital landscape like hulking towers made of oily black stone, smelling of sulphur, heralded by the blacksmith sound of steel being forged for war. There is desperate nostalgia for a time when it was not so, and an acknowledgement of our collective, tacit acceptance that we have no plan in place to tear down these structures. That we are instead making our peace with algorithmic influence, surveillance, rampant misinformation and the breakdown of a social order that once simply seemed like human nature. Turns out human nature can be bought and sold for a sixty-second video and the feeling you get when your phone lights up.

I could tell you that, when I set out to write it, the purpose of this book was to tell some stories about OCD and intrusive thoughts and what it felt like to lose my mind. Stories about friends and family and the narrow margins by which the people I've loved have saved my life. To write about the desperate need for attention and adoration and visibility and the paralysing fear that comes with getting exactly what you asked for. To try to figure out, if I can, what made me the way I am, what makes us the way we are, and where, if anywhere, we're supposed to go from there.

But so much more than that, this book has one purpose – a purpose that unifies it with all such books published throughout history. That is, of course, to be stolen by a tech giant so it can be fed into the gaping maw of a large language model and used to train a generative AI programme to only be kind of wrong when you ask it how many cubic feet of water are in an Olympic-sized swimming pool or to correct your undergraduate thesis for spelling errors.

That and the desperate, terrible, inexcusable egotism to think that it's my writing that you should read. That my thoughts are uniquely worthy of your consideration. That it should be this book that is gifted to hard-to-buy-for relatives across Ireland at Christmastime so they can smile politely and wonder to themselves, *Who the hell is Carl Kinsella?*

I don't have much of an answer for that question besides: I'm the guy whose book you're reading and, if you keep reading, then you may end up figuring it out more than I've managed to yet. You may figure out something else entirely.

It is a profound privilege to publish a book, and its only true purpose is the hope that you, the reader, get something – anything at all – out of it. Thank you for reading.

All my love,

Carl

Excuses, Excuses

DO YOU EVER miss your old brain? You know, your pre-broadband brain. Your dial-up brain. I can barely even remember mine.

I made the uninformed choice to become a part of the World Wide Web when I was eleven years old. With the permission of my mother, I signed up for a vBulletin message board dedicated to the discussion of the 'A Series of Unfortunate Events' children's book series. We had a desktop computer in our house but no internet connection, so the only chance I ever got to browse the Web back then was in my aunt Cathy's computer room. This was back when computers still had entire rooms to themselves, meaning that a Dell

Inspiron 9100 in 2004 was probably living about as well or better than the average Irish renter now. My decision to join that message board to read and share theories as to the fate of the Baudelaire orphans would prove formative. The message board was shuttered only a year or two later, but its effect on me would prove to be irreversible (at least thus far). I had tasted the approval of strangers on the internet, and I no longer cared to go without it.

It's been twelve years now since I set up my Twitter account, and it disturbs me greatly to think that significantly more time has passed between then and now than passed between me setting up that message-board account in my aunt's back room under my mother's supervision and joining Twitter, decidedly not under my mother's supervision. Apparently, we are all now obligated to qualify each mention of Twitter with something like 'which has since rebranded as X', but I don't particularly want to do that. I would love to say this is for some principled, highfalutin reason. That Twitter was more of an idea than a platform, and that when Elon Musk bought it, it changed on an ontological level, and so it would be inaccurate to refer to the Twitter of the past as 'X'. That's not why I'm not going to call it X. I'm not going to call it X because it's a stupid name for a platform, and Elon Musk can get fucked as well, while we're on the subject.

I quit Twitter in late 2024 after its adoptive owner Musk signalled his support for the German far-right party AfD shortly before one of their sympathisers ploughed his car into a crowd of people in a Christmas market in Magdeburg. It was a tragic, though arbitrary, trigger. I'd been trying to get off Twitter for longer than that. For years, I had been dependent on the app for validation, entertainment, information. Since signing up in October 2013, I tweeted an average of eighteen times a day until I stopped last December. Eighteen times a day. I don't even have eighteen thoughts a day. But the reason I undertook this aberrant behaviour is that I was so handsomely rewarded for it. By 2022, I'd accumulated no fewer than 30,000 followers. A legion of people to reassure me that I was funny and insightful, that my public pronouncements were astute and morally correct. To me, every new day on Twitter felt like the moment you put a euro in the coin slot of a pool table and push it and the enormous, earth-shifting *shlock* sound of the slate releasing the balls, the sound of a game beginning anew. A monsoon of coins raining down into the steel tray of a Las Vegas slot machine. When you make a joke that lands, that travels … It must be how C-3PO felt when the Ewoks started worshipping him in *Return of the Jedi*. I can honestly say I don't remember what my brain was like before it.

If you've spent a lot of time on Twitter then I don't need to tell you about it, but, if you're normal, there are a few things you need to understand. One of the most important principles of Twitter was the idea that each day had a 'main character'. This was a seemingly unbreakable cycle wherein at least one person on earth would wake up and tweet something so regrettable that it would be shared far and wide, elevating whichever poor schmuck was foolish enough to arouse the wrath of the masses. Twitter, even at its very best, was a wrathful place. Modern digital platforms are not built for the kind of pro-social behaviour that holds so much of the real world in place, you see. They're built to encourage users – through simple tricks like colours and buttons and the satisfying stretching of the ego that comes from seeing your numbers go up (followers, likes, retweets, whatever) – to make themselves as visible as possible. To 'put' 'themselves' 'out there', as it were. In the case of Twitter, that could mean anything from posting pictures of your asshole to a detailed fifty-tweet thread explaining the impact of tariffs on the global economy. Some users specialise in both. Or, just like in the classroom, you can win attention by relentlessly making jokes even though at least half of everyone probably wants you to stop so they can get on with the lesson. Something like: Hey girl, are you the treoracha and ceisteanna a ghabhann le Cuid A of my scrúidpháipéar? Cos I want to lay you anois go cúramach. One of my more underrated pieces, if you ask me.

Regular Twitter users – users who 'hung out' on Twitter the same way teenagers hang around outside a newsagent's on their bikes intimidating the elderly, just a place to be, just something to do – will remember many main characters from over the years. There was the American man who, in the middle of a gun debate after a mass shooting in the United States, had demanded to know what he was supposed to do to protect his land should *30–50 feral hogs* ever come stampeding across it. People took the piss out of him for a full twenty-four hours, not conceding until years later that he'd actually kind of had a point. There was 'Bean Dad' – a podcast host (once again, American) who'd taken to his timeline to boast that he'd made his nine-year-old daughter struggle for hours to open a can of beans to teach her resilience. Boy, people did not like that. There was one woman who was raked over the coals because of an entirely innocuous tweet in which she expressed love for her partner and spoke of how the two of them would enjoy drinking coffee in the garden together. This did not sufficiently speak to the misery in which most Twitter users apparently live their lives, and so she was thrown into an oubliette or something. I forget.

Mercifully, and despite my tens of thousands of tweets, I never reached the status of main character. I'd never have been able to handle that kind of pressure. And the way I know that about myself is because there was one time I came really close. That was in August 2021, when I started what came to be known as an online disinformation campaign to convince people that the Luas, Dublin's tram service, is free. But we'll come back to that shortly.

I'm ashamed of the first time I went viral. This came five years earlier, in the latter half of 2016. The first reason for that shame is pretty simple and has little to do with the substance of the viral content itself. Like many Irish people, I share the belief that it is a terrible sin to wish to be seen, let alone applauded. Thanks for buying my book, by the way.

The second reason is a little more specific to the content itself. It was a joke I'd posted about Harry Potter, making fun of how the Hogwarts house system sorts kids into four brackets, which I described in the tweet as 'brave, smart, evil and miscellaneous'. It was a joke I'd told a thousand times in my mind and a deeply unoriginal observation. This was 2016, after all. Jokes about Harry Potter were pretty hackneyed by then. There'd been entire universes built out of Harry Potter parodies, YouTube videos that were as well known to some corners of the internet as the series itself.

A Very Potter Musical, those Potter Puppet Pal things. All this to say that I didn't think, as I sent that tweet between stripping off my gear from five-a-side and getting into the shower, that I was about to break the internet (or make a small incision into some unimportant crevice of its flesh, as proved to be the case). This was, however, before the cultural darkening that has set in over the years since. Back then, people were still laughing at celebrities reading mean tweets, having their minds blown by *Hamilton* and tolerating Carpool Karaoke in an act of inspiring non-violence. Though J.K. Rowling had yet to take up her mantle as arguably the world's foremost anti-trans activist, I certainly have felt much after-the-fact shame for directing any attention to her work for quite some time. If there is anything to mitigate that shame it's that there is probably nobody on earth who learned about Harry Potter through my tweets.

When I woke up the next morning, the tweet had amassed over 10,000 likes. I had notifications on my phone telling me my tweet had been trending in Canada, in parts of California, all over the place. I was getting retweeted by the little girl who played Matilda, who was, by that point, actually twenty-nine years old. If you've ever gone viral, you'll know that these weird and specific updates – that a certain location is really buzzing off your joke, that some meme aggregation page has stolen it, cropped out your username and is sharing it as their own, or that some famous or powerful person knows who you are all of sudden – are par for the course. It stops being exciting almost instantly, and becomes a chore immediately after that. The first time a mentally healthy person goes viral on a certain platform, they will mute notifications for that app for the sake of their sanity and their battery and never look back.

I did not do that. After this brush with attention – true attention, the attention of tens of thousands – I set about spending the entirety of my twenties so desperate for validation and reassurance that, before long, I was thinking in tweets. I was dreaming in tweets. My followers had practically doubled over the course of one night – still only a measly 1,400, mind you – and because Twitter is (or was) a platform about sharing and being reshared, this came with a multiplier effect. The more followers you have, the more followers will follow, and eventually you and your thoughts are followed around everywhere by tens of thousands of people whom you don't know, whose stability you can't vouch for and whose judgement you can't trust. And any time you put anything out there into the world, those people are watching. This is something the normals tend to overlook about having an audience. After all, imagine any group of a hundred people and ask yourself, on average, how many of them are freaks. Imagine how many of the hundred just plain won't like you or your vibe or your face or whatever. Think about what percentage will know more than you about whatever you're talking about either through study or lived experience, ready to legitimately put you back in your box. Now, imagine you've just said something that's about to be seen by 100,000 people. The maths are quite simple. Before long, you find yourself answering your own thoughts in the voice of your cruellest and keenest detractors. A spiral of second-, third-, fourth-guessing yourself, like one mirror facing another, locked into the realisation that whether you are telling a joke or making some earnest observation, you will not capture your subject cleanly enough to get away scot-free from critique. If enough people see a thing, then some of them will be pissed off by that thing. Doesn't remotely matter what the thing is. The first principle of woodwork, besides don't wear a tie that can get caught in the reciprocating saw, is to measure twice and cut once. The business of going viral is different. Measure never. Cut indiscriminately.

The transition from a mostly physical existence where one's social milieu might include a handful of friends and family, a smattering of co-workers, the people you might pass on the bus or in the pub, acquaintances from social clubs to a digital realm where anyone can access you at any time and you can end up as the 'main character' – paraded before the village like a goat on a float or a jester in the guillotine – has transformed the potential for personal ruin. It has fundamentally altered the equation of potentiality. Now, you can post a video of yourself online and change your life by accident. You can become famous because people like the way you say a certain word, because your gimmick, your schtick, is exactly what was needed on a certain day. The one-two punch of smartphones and digital platforms has made it so that every moment of your life is overburdened with the potential for enormous change, in a way that used to be reserved for major life events.

Having a child, for example, is widely accepted as something that will necessarily change your life, and it is therefore unsurprising when it inevitably does. Bo-ring. Other inflection points are less predictable, less obviously laden with fatedness. Like if you were to cross Wexford Street because you spotted someone standing outside Whelan's whom you'd been avoiding for the last few months. And when you get across the street you remember that you need to buy some Piriton for your hay fever. It's August and you're eighteen years old and you weigh less than 60 kilograms and you're wearing red sweatpants from Penneys and an extra-small white T-shirt with a big Superman S on it that is also from Penneys. You are so lost in the thrill of having so seamlessly dodged unwelcome human interaction, you don't really question it when you file into the pharmacy between a guy wearing a motorcycle helmet and a second guy who is also wearing a motorcycle helmet. In fact, so oblivious are you to what is about to happen, you hold the door open for the second erstwhile motorcyclist.

Approximately five seconds after the door closes behind him, the second helmeted man, taller and thicker than you, tells you to get behind the counter, and you quickly realise you are now, even in the absolute best-case scenario, a witness to a robbery. It's sort of like what Carl Sagan said about how if you want to make an apple pie from scratch, you must first invent the universe. Only in this case, the apple pie is an event that has left me mildly but indelibly scarred, and the creation of the universe is my decision to cross the street. What I learned about myself over the course of that robbery is that I'm the kind of guy who, if told by a robber to get on the floor, will get on the floor. No questions asked. When I run the memory back in my mind now, I do have a vague sense that I may have asked, 'Can't I just, like, leave?' I'm pretty sure I didn't actually say that, but I can guarantee you my overall performance was precisely that unheroic.

The robbery itself, in action, was a grotesque affair, and undoubtedly traumatic for the two women who were staffing the pharmacy. At one point, one of the men alluded to having a gun, but I certainly never saw one. Had I, then I would have crashed out on the spot and the guy would have had to shoot me just to calm me down. One time I was telling a friend this story and he said, 'Ah, he didn't have a gun', and when I asked how he could be so sure, he said, 'In those situations, if you have a gun, you show it.' Obviously my friend, who has spent his entire life unarmed, hadn't a fucking clue what he was talking about but I agreed with him nevertheless. Still, when you're lying on the linoleum behind the counter of a pharmacy, watching two anonymous men threaten two women, lying there like a eunuch in your Superman T-shirt, realising you've got a face that screams *Please make an example of me*, it does change the way you think about the world.

I'd been mugged before, but this was a step up from my past experiences. The muggings I'd been party to by that very early stage in my life had always offered some room either for negotiation or for sprinting in the opposite direction as fast as I could. I could have even screamed 'I am being mugged' if the situation had grown truly hairy. That is to say, mugging was unpleasant, but it had never made me feel truly helpless.

But, inadvertently locking myself into a dangerous situation because I wouldn't risk a conversation with an acquaintance and don't possess the necessary skills of visual observation to notice that I have sandwiched myself between two men who are obviously about to rob a pharmacy? That has an effect. It wasn't quite a conscious decision on my part, but it was dumb enough to be negligent, and that's nearly the same thing. Maybe it's an experience like that which makes you seek the illusory safety of the internet. Who's to say? I'm wary of ascribing too much significance to this event, and warier still of dismissing it entirely.

There is nothing unique about this story besides that it happened to me, but things like this happen to people every day. Things that shouldn't matter, decisions that should be of no consequence at all, often reshape our lives. Ideally, we are not wearing an extra-small Superman T-shirt when it happens. After the helmeted men had left the pharmacy with however much money they'd cobbled together from the till and some sacks that were kept in what seemed to be some kind of safe, I waited for the gardaí to show up, gave my statement and my contact information and, naturally, never heard anything about the incident ever again. Somehow, amid the madness, I did get my hands on some Piriton (did I … steal them?), but as I turned the corner and made for St Stephen's

Green I threw the unopened box into a large commercial bin as though that would cleanse me of the experience.

That happened in 2011, probably one of the last years when you still had to at least cross the street to end up in a potentially ruinous situation. The internet had yet to build up enough steam for a full churn. There were very few 'main characters' at that point, and even they were usually people who had done something so embarrassing in real life that it had made it onto the internet, rather than the other way round. This was four years before Jon Ronson published his book *So You've Been Publicly Shamed* – perhaps the first mainstream work to highlight the notion that the increased visibility afforded to us by popular social-media platforms was a double-edged sword, and that the more we suppress our true selves in favour of the broadcasted, live-streamed, tweeted self, the higher the jeopardy.

Maybe you don't feel as though much really changed with the advent of social media, at least with respect to the damage we can do to ourselves. Sure, you could have always slipped in the shower, burned your arm when cooking with oil, fallen down the stairs or whatever else like that. But there was a time when, at the very least, the four walls of one's bedroom felt sanctified and safe. Amniotic and impenetrable. You could roll down the blinds like Gandalf throwing the sleeve of his robe over the Palantir, a curtain over the whole globe, and experience the unconscious and unheralded relief of being truly hidden. It's not like that anymore. Ruining your life has never required less effort, premeditation or forethought. You could ruin your life right now. You could put this book down, open up whatever social-media account you've got the most friends or followers on and just go for it. I won't tell you how to go about it, there's no one way to skin a cat and there are plenty of people whose example you can follow. Even if you've only got an audience of a few hundred, you are presently in possession of the otherworldly power to reach almost everyone you know in an instant. And whether it's on purpose or by accident, you could make them hate your guts just as fast.

The good news, though, is that 'ruining your life' has also never been a better pathway to get rich. If you don't embarrass easily and are prepared to withstand the hatred of 100,000 people who either idly or actively want you dead, there really is no limit to what you can achieve. You know there's a lady in Minnesota named Shiloh Hendrix who was caught on camera directing a racial slur towards a black child in a playground, and after a few hours of well-earned internet shaming, she managed to raise $800,000 on a crowdfunding website under the title 'Help Me Protect My Family'? That's

$800,000 for being captured in the commission of one of the most reprehensible acts imaginable. The incentives to behave monstrously have never been higher; all we ask is that you let us watch.

In another example of a moment recorded on a phone and cast into our attending jaws like chum to sea serpents, a twenty-one-year-old Alabamian girl named Haliey Welch was asked on camera while on a night out how to make a guy go crazy in bed, and she gave some half-baked advice about what to do when giving head. As a token of our gratitude for her sage advice, we made her one of the most famous women in the world, instantly, giving her the name 'Hawk Tuah' in honour of the onomatopoeia she'd used to describe the act of spitting on, as she called it, 'that thang'. Within weeks, Welch had one of the most popular podcasts on the market. She has millions of followers on Instagram. She scammed hundreds of morons out of their money by selling a cryptocurrency memecoin that instantly lost all of its value, and then she disappeared off the face of the internet for weeks when her fans realised they'd been had. As of May 2025, Welch is being sued in a class-action lawsuit and has been investigated by the FBI and SEC. This is presumably fantastic news for her brand, because the longer it drags on, the more access we give Welch to the mines of our attention. Netflix or some other streaming giant will almost undoubtedly make a documentary about her – or a whole docuseries. Welch, like many of us, is a participant in the attention economy. A merchant, if you will. She has her stall, and I have mine, and perhaps you have your own.

Maybe the most dangerous thing about the attention economy is that, for now, the attention that matters only comes from one source, which is people. 'Success' is entirely contingent on winning the notice of people, the more the better. The reason this is so dangerous is that people are dangerous to begin with, and the online forums in which they congregate have a habit of making even the most straightforward exchange of information feel like a cockfight being watched by 10,000 drunken gamblers.

There are, at best, content-moderation rules to which even the more responsible platforms barely adhere. Even before its Elon Musk era, Twitter was not a platform that stringently enforced its own rules. When tens of thousands of people encounter an idea – any idea – all at once, some of those people are going to be really weird about it. If you ask anyone who has ever gone viral for any reason, they will tell you the very same thing. It's worse if you're a woman because, within those tens of thousands, there will be an enormous cohort who will behave abominably not only about the substance of your idea but about your physical appearance, your marital status, whether or not you have children. In many cases, this is accompanied by threats of sexual violence from men – some anonymous, some so secure in their sense of impunity that they have no problem attaching their name and likeness to this harassment.

And those are just the malevolent weirdos. There are benevolent weirdos too. In Twitter parlance, benevolent weirdos are usually relegated to a caste known as 'Reply Guys' – men, usually older than whomever it is they are replying to, perhaps attempting to live out some fantasy in which they can appeal to the kind of women who ignored them in their teens and twenties. 'Reply Guys' seem to be possessed of that same essence that seems to make uncles such reliably strange people. A supportiveness not untouched by sleaze, and a great propensity to respond to your tweet with a follow-up observation from a perspective that you do not share but that is not worth going out of your way to challenge. 'Benevolent' might actually be a bit strong – weirdos about whom you feel neutral.

So sick are these platforms, and so sick is the outside world they are remaking in their own image, that at times it seems the only way to use them right is to misuse them. There's a comforting, cathartic logic to this. Hey, if all of the most powerful people in the world can hop online and lie and prevaricate and grandstand without any fear of consequence, then surely it is as much our right to do the same. Unfortunately, the platforms don't care whether you're using them or misusing them. It's all the same as long as they can keep you on their app, looking at ads, willingly turning over your personal data. It's the attention economy, stupid.

Do you want to guess how many tweets there are on Twitter that refer to it as a 'hellsite'? How many accounts have tweeted threatening to kill owner Elon Musk, or Jack Dorsey before him? There are people who profess to hate Twitter who can sooner imagine the end of the internet than actually extracting themselves from the situation. And I don't say that out of a place of judgement, but sincere empathy.

The attention economy truly kicked into gear with the 'pivot to video' that occurred in the mid-2010s. Facebook, now Meta, told all of the digital publishers – the Buzzfeeds, the Huffington Posts, the Vices, not to mention the organisations I have spent my entire professional life working for – who relied entirely upon the followings they had built on Facebook, that these followers would no longer be shown articles in their Newsfeed to the same degree as they had been. Instead, the algorithm would prioritise videos. People weren't reading anymore, we were told. It took a couple of years, but the result was an attempt by journalists and organisations who had carved out their niche by relying on the public's tapeworm-like hunger for quizzes that would tell them which Lady Gaga backing dancer they were to retool their approach for people with even *less* of an attention span. The 'pivot to video' was a cataclysmic blow to many of the main upstart publications of the early 2010s, including the likes of Vice and Buzzfeed. Instead, the actual 'pivot to video' came a few years later, fulfilled by the public themselves.

In the eighteenth century, an English philosopher named Jeremy Bentham proposed the idea of the panopticon – an architectural innovation that was intended to make institutions, such as prisons, easier to monitor. The design consists of a rotunda with an inspection dock at its centre from which a warden can sit on his spinny chair and create the perception that all occupants in the prison are visible – surveillable – at all times. The kind of structure that has been built for us, here in the twenty-first century, is like an omni-panopticon. All of us at once both prisoners and wardens, trapped in some Escheresque structure wherein we can instantaneously tap into the lives of virtually anyone else on earth, or at least a valiant performance of it, an imitation of life. We can also do whatever we please to draw the searchlight to ourselves, beckon our fellow prisoners to cheer for us from their own lonely cells or to turn prison guard and descend upon us with truncheons. And here's the thing: until you hit send on whatever it is you want to put out there, you really have no idea which it's going to be.

Bored and underemployed of a Thursday afternoon in August 2021, it occurred to me that one of my eighteen or so tweets for the day should be this:

> A long-term goal of mine has been to lead a disinformation campaign which claims that the Luas is free until enough people believe it that they have no choice but to give in and make the Luas is free. So if anyone ever asks you, remember: the Luas is free.

So, the tweet itself. First things first, the errant 'is' between 'Luas' and 'free' at the end of the first sentence makes me wish I were dead and will drive me crazy until the end of time. And now it's immortalised in a book. Just great. Secondly, I didn't expect all that much of a response to this tweet, at least in part because I'd already tweeted the exact same thing years earlier and nobody cared. That the idea was met with such an explosion of interest this second time around reflects little more than the parallel vagaries inherent to both digital-platform algorithms and the human soul. Something that does not interest us one day might captivate us the next, though it probably helps if people have been primed by roughly eighteen months of pandemic-induced cabin fever.

In the spirit of a true disinformation campaign, I hung back over the coming hours. Typically, it had been my wont to fervently retweet any praise that ever came my way. If an article I'd written had done especially well and people were lining up to tell me I'd 'hit the nail on the head', I would perform like a clapping seal and retweet that endorsement to my own followers. *Look how funny everyone agrees I am, you guys.* This time, however, I tried to stay true to the idea of a disinformation campaign and fade into the background, going full *éminence grise*. The idea proposed by my tweet gathered more steam – a frustrating metaphor to rely upon when writing about a tram, but whatever – than I'd anticipated. By far. It quickly escaped my own sphere of influence and thereby any semblance of control I might have exercised over it. It was only a matter of time before the normals got their hands on it. The normals, those folk still unpoisoned by the seventeen layers of irony that over- and underpin virtually any sentiment that thrives on a landscape such as Twitter. Ah, the naive, blissful normals. How would they take it?

Within forty-eight hours of the tweet being posted, I started getting text messages from friends telling me their parents had asked them if the Luas had actually been made free like they'd seen online. I was a little stunned by that, but only for a minute. How many people had been exposed to it by then? 50,000? More? Many of whom would have seen it without context. By now, thousands more Twitter users had joined in, coming up with their own take on the tweet, obscuring its origins. Making it seem, for want of a better word, real. Not really my doing, I told myself. I'd always felt like I had a large degree of plausible deniability in my favour. After all, I'd called it a disinformation campaign in my original tweet. If you're planning a real disinformation campaign, you don't tell people that's what you're doing. But after only two days, that's exactly what it had become.

A more savvy, less terrified acolyte of the attention economy would have seized on the opportunity. They'd have trademarked it, made badges, made tote bags, made T-shirts, made any money at all. I, on the other hand, was turning down radio interviews out of anxiety. I felt like a kid at a birthday party who'd gathered all his aunts and uncles in a circle so they could watch me do a cool new trick, and instead I'd whacked my head off the corner of the kitchen counter and now wanted everyone to stop looking as I quietly bled out.

The excitement over the 'Luas is free' thing had not died down and, instead, had intensified well beyond any of my many past experiences of virality. My brain had kicked into gear and began turning over the only question that ever seems to truly rouse it from its slumber: 'How will this hurt me?' It had got altogether out of hand. Dara Ó Briain was tweeting about it. The official Dublin Airport Twitter account was tweeting about it. Articles ran with headlines like: 'Dublin Twitter users react as people are questioning if the Luas is free' and subheadings like: 'It seems the joke has gone a bit too far as "the Luas is free" has been trending on Twitter.' I had long since stopped enjoying myself. Few things give me as much pleasure as one of my jokes going too far, but usually there aren't so many people watching. And besides, my anxiety was still trying to figure out how exactly this whole escapade was going to ruin my life. *Please, Dara Ó Briain, please stop tweeting about it. Can't you see I'm in danger?*

The one comfort I took from the onslaught of 'Luas is Free' tweets was the rationalisation that it could be seen as some kind of mass peaceful protest against Ireland's lousy and over-expensive public transport infrastructure. If that had been my aim, however, I'd have targeted Dublin Bus. If I ever launch a campaign against Dublin Bus, it will not have the frivolity of the 'Luas is free' campaign. It will be a video of me pulling out a fingernail with a pliers and holding it up the camera so Dublin Bus know what they've put me through. I can only speak anecdotally, but the Luas has simply never caused me to wonder whether I am actually a danger to myself and others in the way that a 49 bus disappearing from Dublin Bus' oxymoronically named Real Time Information app does.

But back to how my little joke about the Luas was going to ruin my life. One of the first fantasies that followed this line of thinking was the idea that people at large would not only be truly fooled by this 'campaign', but they would be caught en masse on Luases across Dublin not having paid their way onto the tram. Apprehended by those orange-coated ticket inspectors – plumage designed to warn us of predators – or worse still, the Luas security forces. If you have never ridden the Luas, then you will not know about the Luas security guys. I don't know who pays them, all I know is that they are – almost universally – around 6 foot 5 and dressed like they could, at any moment, be deployed to Abbottabad to take down an al-Qaeda splinter cell. Forget An Garda Síochána or the Defence Forces, the Luas security guys are the only force I would consider capable of executing a violent coup d'état or a military junta in Ireland. Anyway, my fear was that there would be a kind of Execute Order 66 moment in which my fellow freeriders would be tackled to the ground by these heavies, and that, under duress, they would give me up. I imagined some Twitter-addicted twenty-something in a garda station interrogation room illuminated only by one unshaded bulb swinging from the ceiling. 'It was Kinsella, he put us up to it! He told us it was free!'

I scanned the Irish statute book to see if I'd broken any laws, and from what I could tell I hadn't, though I continued to live in fear that I would somehow be caught up in a class-action lawsuit where all those who had suffered the €150 fine decided that I'd pied-pipered them into a life of fare-dodging and that the whole thing was my fault. I started to do some calculations to see how much I'd owe. Say a thousand people tried to pin the blame for their fare-dodging on me, that was €150,000 I'd never be able to pay back for starters. And that's before they got me on the punitive damages for all the distress I'd caused.

I simply didn't have the stomach to maximise the attention that was on me. At my time of maximum leverage, I was struck by the terror I had wrought – look on my works, ye mighty, and despair – and turned tail. The few interviews I did accept, I accepted only in the form of questions being emailed to me, for fear that if I spoke aloud I would lose control of my tongue and say something that incriminated me ahead of the trials and lawsuits I assumed were pending.

An extract from an interview with JOE.ie, originally published on 10 August 2021:

Q: Have you seen any negative reactions to it or from it?

Carl: Yeah, but that's pretty much par for the course when so many people interact with something. If a joke gets done to death or ends up all over somebody's timeline, I think it's pretty understandable that they won't like it. I mean, I'm sure loads of people don't like it for all sorts of reasons. They're probably right too. At the end of the day, it's probably not a great thing that something I've thought about for all of five seconds ends up reaching loads of people.

Important stuff. Philosophical. You can see why I felt I had to choose my words carefully. One of the more negative reactions I saw to my tweet was that it would actually increase the amount of security on the Luas, thereby further carceralising the whole process and putting people in further danger of being harassed or hassled for not paying. The suggestion was that I had broken some kind of *omertà* agreement that had been in place, that we'd all been not paying for the Luas in peace and now I'd come along to spoil the fun. It was a complaint that took a level of contrivance that even I would be proud of, and the idea that Transdev or Transport Infrastructure Ireland or the Department of Transport were about to pay more salaries or more overtime in order to address an 'online event' was about as likely as my own fantasies of being hauled before a court for what I'd said.

Or so I thought, until it turned out that staff at Transport Infrastructure Ireland actually had raised the matter with the gardaí, according to an article from *The Journal* at the start of that September.

Transport officials contacted gardaí over a hoax Twitter account after a joke about Dublin's Luas service being free to use went viral last month. Staff from Transport Infrastructure Ireland (TII) contacted An Garda Síochána's fraud section, as well as Twitter and Instagram, after a fake account purporting to be an official Luas account tweeted the joke.

All at once, I was shocked and relieved and disappointed. I could tell from the reaction to the news story that people were pretty unimpressed that a semi-state body would try to engage the guards in a self-evidently non-criminal act. I was, however, a little deflated to learn that the tweet that had prompted the outreach to the gardaí was not one of my own, but a follow-up from someone else who had taken it a step further and created a fake Luas Twitter account and used it to emancipate those slithery, silver beauties from their fare plans. To use a historical parallel, I was sort of like the J.D. Salinger to their Mark David Chapman. Which, by extension, I suppose, in this particular analogy, would make the Luas and its parent company John Lennon. Although relieved that my fears of prosecution had abated, I was indignant that any organisation would stoop so low as to almost enter the realms of what my delusional mind thought was plausible.

In the few weeks that had passed since that first weekend when the joke had taken off, my usual routine had resumed – whatever I had been anxious about had been overtaken by some other more pressing and similarly delusional worry, and I had ceased even to think about the previous concern that I had once believed threatened my very existence on this earth. Sort of like rearranging the deckchairs on the *Titanic* only, in this case, the *Titanic* wasn't sinking – the captain just thinks it is because he's experiencing severe delusions at the wheel. In this case, the rearranging of the deckchairs isn't so much useless as just a nuisance to everyone else trying to enjoy their post-Edwardian Atlantic boat adventure. Can you guys remember what I was talking about? Oh yeah, the Luas.

In light of all this, I've never especially liked taking credit for starting the 'Luas is Free' gag. Even drawing attention to it now feels sort of gauche. Like a graffiti artist with his balaclava pulled up around his head standing next to a frescoed cinder block wall stopping passers-by to ask them what they think of his work. There's also something especially lame about referring to online events as if they are 'real'. What does it mean for something to 'happen' online, anyway? There is a sterility to events that originate online, because nothing truly originates online. To think of something as originating online separates it from its elemental nature, from the truth that, at some point this idea came from a living, breathing person, some tangle of flesh and blood and bone and consciousness, sitting on his bed in his apartment overlooking the Old Kent Road, more or less unemployed, thinking, *Do you know what would be funny?*

For years, I have suffered the humiliation of having my online life rooted through by my friends in the fleshworld. It's unseemly. Incongruent. Talking about the things people say to the internet from beneath their duvet … It should be beneath us. Imagine you'd been tinkering in your back garden and invented an appliance or activity of virtually no value whatsoever. Imagine you strapped a Go-Pro to your lawnmower and began uploading weekly updates of the grass being cut from the perspective of the machine. You might find it amusing for whatever reason, and you might share it with your friends, not because you have any intention of selling the patent to Lockheed Martin or because you want a brand deal from the lawnmower people. You know it won't make you famous or make you any money. Truth be told, you're actually a little embarrassed that it brings you any joy at all.

Then, imagine that several times a year, your friends or acquaintances or co-workers introduce you to people at parties as 'the guy who came up with the POV Lawnmower'. You really don't know just how blank a stare can truly be until you've been introduced to someone as 'the guy who came up with the Luas is free thing'. Most people haven't even heard about it! And many of the people who heard about it at the time have forgotten it ever happened! And yet, I have to stand there while some thirtysomething who has snorted more interesting things than 'the Luas is Free' in the last hour alone decides how polite to be about this unsolicited and overbearing introduction. The worst-case scenario is when someone is both unimpressed and disbelieving which means, for the sake of my own honour, I have to clarify that yes I did start 'the Luas is Free' but no, I'm not especially proud of it. Don't ever tell anyone I'm proud of it. Tell them it was me, sure, I don't want anyone else getting the credit. But don't tell people I'm proud of it. I've done cooler things. I swear to God, I've done cooler things.

A few years after it all went down, my friend James asked me how I 'felt' about what he referred to as 'the whole "Luas is free" thing'. He wasn't any more specific than that at first, but I knew what he was saying. He's a comedian. A weird one. I don't fully understand the intention of everything he does in his sets, but I admire what he does. Long pauses, building tension with the audience. The kind of thing I'm not built for, the kind of thing I do the opposite of – my immediate-gratification approach of thoughtlessly composing half-jokes stripped of all context and poured carelessly into the void like emptying a kettle into a river as it rushes by. While I didn't know quite what he wanted from me, I could discern the clause that he had magnanimously lopped off. What he was asking was, 'How do you feel about the whole "Luas is Free" thing being so popular, given that it's not actually funny?' He interrupted my humming and hawing to help me out, asking more clearly this time, 'Why do you think people find it funny?'

Now, with some time and space to think about that question, I experience a sort of psychedelic and transcendental cacophony where I can hear disembodied voices in my ear rasping in a sort of death rattle about whether I left the immersion on, warning me that mammy will fetch the wooden spoon if I've forgotten to take the chicken out of the freezer, unless she's distracted because there's grand drying out this evening. Sure, either way, the brittle, spectral voice echoes, we can make up over a spice bag or a chicken fillet roll. The kind of jokes that somehow seem to resonate among tens of thousands of rapt short-form video consumers despite having no actual humour involved besides words and ideas that we recognise from our own lives. Is that all 'the Luas is free' is? Is it even that? If I died right now, this Luas thing would probably be part of my obituary. A big part of it, probably. That's if I get an obituary. One time I asked my friends whether they thought RTÉ or *The Irish Times* would report on it if I died. They all said no.

I know why *I* – in the very first instance – found it funny to make my little joke about the Luas being free, but I've never been entirely clear about what other people found so amusing about it. When I sent that tweet, the very best I could have hoped for was that the Department of Transport or Transdev had to issue a statement in which they said something along the lines of: 'Please do not listen to Carl Kinsella.' It was not, therefore, a venture entirely free of ego. Actually, as I tot up the figures now, it was probably around 99 per cent ego. I had daydreamed about a scenario in which staffers for then-minister for transport Eamon Ryan had to compile a dossier on me in case he was asked at some press briefing about my mischievous endeavours. Notoriety of exactly this kind has always appealed to me, to be known as someone who should not be listened to on any matter under any circumstances. Regarded by all as a rascal. That RTÉ's captured audience across the country would tune in to the *Six-One News* after the Angelus and be faced with Micheál Martin's grave expression, pleading with people not to heed the advice of this scallywag. So why did anybody else find it funny?

I'm not sure it was funny at first. There are some things that aren't funny until they hit a certain scale. Andy Kaufman's Mighty Mouse routine isn't funny if you do it in front of your relatives at Christmas, but if you get on *Saturday Night Live* and use your fifteen minutes of fame to do something that dumb? That's funny. One guy saying the Luas is free is not especially funny – but thousands of people saying the Luas is free? The Luas people having to come out and deny that the Luas is free? Transport Infrastructure Ireland calling the guards over it? That's quite good. And none of that had anything to do with me. As I mentioned, my involvement was limited after the original tweet was out there. I did, regrettably, respond to one tweet by a presumably overworked and beleaguered person manning the Luas Twitter account that weekend. The account had begun fielding questions from those who had evidently been led astray by the growing deluge of seemingly unironic tweets praising the Luas for being such a great, free service that was free and did not cost money. Sally, the name used by whomever was on call for the Luas social media that day, was batting these people away left and right. I certainly didn't help her cause when I responded to one of her tweets desperately insisting that a valid ticket was needed to ride the Luas with: I can't believe they're trying to introduce fares to the Luas. It should remain free.

There is not enough room in this book for me to adequately explain the network of digital ecosystems that comprise Twitter, nor would I have the expertise to do so. And if there is any Irish person who should have the expertise to do so, it's almost certainly me. Unfortunately, trying to describe Twitter as an ecosystem would be like trying to describe a beach by detailing every grain of sand, and how the colour of each grain may change under the sunlight, and how each grain exists in relation to every other grain. To have even the faintest chance of understanding the nature of Twitter and its happenings, we would need an Attenboroughesque figure to speak to us soothingly as we watch footage of an unsuspecting forty-six-year-old man tweet foolhardily about his parenting habits only to become Twitter's 'main character' for the day as he's torn limb from limb by people who may well believe what they are saying, but are compromised, their positions automatically contaminated and untenable, by the ecosystem itself. Why should anyone believe what you say when there is such a clear ulterior incentive for you to say it? Every tweet, every post of any kind into the ether carries with it this hope that the author will experience the kind of divination that a gambler gets from watching a jockey whip his horse, all of us galloping for the finish line, neck and neck with everything and nothing in particular all at once.

If we did have a David Attenborough to make equivalent documentaries about these digibiomes, he would not be a beloved figure. We would not brace ourselves every time we hear his name or see a particularly tributary photo of him, for fear he had finally shuffled off this mortal coil. No, if there was anyone out there who understood Twitter on such a forensic level as to be able to truly explain it to the world at large, such a person would rightly be a pariah. An oracle living in a cave who we would only visit when another, more unspeakable evil emerges, like those movies where Godzilla is on our side for some reason.

It is, at least to people of my generation, still rather unchic to be too deeply invested in what's happening inside of your computer and, by extension, your phone, which has also been a computer for the last decade or more. A hangover, perhaps, from the computer-nerd stereotype that was so pervasive in the 1980s and 1990s, when getting anything remotely useful out of a computing system required time and dedication and a vitamin D deficiency. That power has now been Prometheus-ed into our pockets, an otherworldly, nigh-magical force that has been captured and encased in solid-state drives, coursing through steel, brass, bronze, copper, aluminium, zinc, silver and cobalt. An unstoppable stream of information thrumming through undersea cables and beamed invisibly to the heavens and back, all so that we can go online and vaguely suggest that maybe somebody deserves to die because they tweeted something that irritates us.

It is a far cry from what I originally thought computers were for – watching every possible screensaver on Windows 98, trying every possible stock background provided by the operating system, and using MS Paint to draw the Ireland flag. Younger people – the cohort known globally as 'Gen Z', as if there are no other factors in deciding a person's interiority beyond the year they were born – may feel differently. Maybe the concept of a 'computer nerd' no longer exists. The way of the computer nerd has simply become the mode of living for people whose pudgy little fingers pressed greasily upon iPad screens even as babes. But for people my age and older, there is still something pathetic about being overly concerned with the digital world.

It is precisely because events that take place online are seen as lesser — less important, less real, less significant — that there is some stupid pride in creating something that penetrates the real world and forces all of these fleshpeople with their 'real problems' to stop what they're doing and take some degree of notice. Think less *Truth coming from the well armed with her whip to chastise humanity* and more an eldritch abomination emerging from the bottom of the sea after 100,000 millennia of cold and dreamless sleep. A silver-and-purple serpent with me on its back, riding it all the way to hell.

Exile In Dollywood

WHEN I WAS a very young child, the only job I was interested in was that of President of the United States. That should give you some idea of the kind of scumbag you're dealing with here. Five years old, and that was my first instinct? Don't worry, the odds of me passing down these genes get narrower every day.

Maybe if my parents had been firefighters or delivered the post, anything with a uniform, I'd have aspired to something else. Around that time, both of my parents were public servants working for Dublin City Council or, as it was known at the time, the Corporation. And while that did sound pretty badass, like the name of an enemy organisation in a *Mission:*

Impossible film whose affiliation has to be kept vague so as not to unsettle any foreign movie-going markets, I had no idea what it was my parents actually did for work. Seeing as how they didn't conform to any of the cool professions I'd thus far learned about – professional wrestler, Second World War soldier, *Wacky Races* driver – I had to figure out for myself what it was that I was supposed to be.

This was the late 1990s and I'd recently had my first taste of politics when meeting Proinsias De Rossa canvassing outside Lansdowne Road ahead of an Ireland match. I liked his beard, and I liked how the name Proinsias sounded, and I've been paying an unhealthy and unproductive amount of attention to electoral politics ever since.

I don't think, especially between the ages of five and ten, it was my intention to personally wield the power of the executive branch to achieve a specific slate of legislative aims I'd put together in between chewing on the leg of my Action Man and playing football by myself on the green in front of our house. I certainly don't think it was about personally wanting to be Bill Clinton, either. In fact, I have no memory of ever feeling anything for Bill Clinton when I was young. I was upset when his vice-president Al Gore lost the 2000 election, but that was because I knew George W. Bush was accused of stealing it from him, and I knew stealing was wrong, even if the US Supreme Court said it was okay. At that time, I was still a firm adherent to the Ten Commandments as an authority above all else (and in fairness to me, even at the time of writing, there are still at least some Commandments I haven't broken, at least depending on your definition of the word 'covet'). And besides, Gore's pal Clinton was portrayed more sympathetically on *The Simpsons* than George W. Bush's father was.

This was a time when much of Ireland still only had access to a handful of television stations, creating a monocultural captive audience that can, to this day, for better or worse, communicate to one another using quotes, scenes and even still images from *The Simpsons*, almost like hieroglyphs. If I ever have the opportunity to unstack every core memory in my mind and analyse them one by one, I would be especially interested to discover which was the first *Simpsons* joke that made it feel like such an indispensable part of my life. At what point I graduated from thinking Bart was cool because he had a skateboard to blindly enjoying Homer's take on Walter Mondale ('Where's the beef?' No wonder he won Minnesota) or Grampa's claim that he was spanked by Grover Cleveland on two non-consecutive occasions.

I wanted to be President of the United States of America because it had the word 'America' in it, and it stood to reason that the guy who presided over America would be the guy who got to enjoy it the most.

It was 1998 when my parents took me to the States for the first time, to stay in motels in Clearwater and Orlando, meet Mickey Mouse and ride teacups in a heatwave. Before we'd even disembarked the plane, they had purchased for me a small animatronic gorilla with realistic fur and a red-and-white sailor suit. The gorilla could both sing the 'Macarena' and make a plausible attempt at the dance, and I was in love with him. As we alighted, I was struck by a sensation that I don't have a direct memory of but I have a memory of the memory, replenished every time I step off a plane in a country where the sun is hot enough to cook the asphalt, to manipulate the refractive index of the air, turning flat horizons into sine waves as I breathe in the rising benzene, toluene and xylene. That feeling of being somewhere new, of walking down the aisle of a supermarket in a country where the cleaning products they use to disinfect the linoleum are different to those back home. Of seeing TV ads for products you've never even heard of before. The chemically induced rekiltering of the body and brain as they adjust to the sensorial inputs of a new environment.

I remember that holiday the way most of us remember events from our early childhood. A series of still images –

Polaroids that likely bear little resemblance to the experience in and of itself, reality overwritten by a decades spent unconsciously reshaping memories to better fit the life that leans upon them for its justification. I do have a clear memory of being bitten by a fire ant on Clearwater Beach, and the buckle of my jelly sandals cutting into my foot whenever I had to wear them. Same goes for the ear infection I probably picked up from the motel pool, and eating a pancake at Denny's and thinking that the blood-red jam they'd used to give the thing a smiley face had come from inside my ear canal. I remember my parents ordering a pizza the size of a whole table, and I remember my dad taking me to a vending machine while we played mini-golf, and getting me a can of something that to this day I can only describe as like Coke, but more aggressive. I have never tasted anything like it before or since, but in my maturity I'm prepared to accept that this elixir was probably just a regular Dr Pepper, and maybe that's what happens when Dr Pepper hits the tongue of a five-year-old whose forebears likely subsisted on a diet of carrots and stream water for millennia.

I clearly remember us embarking on some kind of novelty pirate-ship experience for children, and this being where I heard and witnessed 'YMCA' for the first time, before eventually giving up on the whole thing because it was too hot. Even so, the pirates kindly gave me a novelty doubloon, which I cherished for much of my childhood, as I did the nautical gorilla who danced the Macarena. I remember watching the American version of *Blue's Clues* on the motel TV, hosted by Steve instead of the usual Kevin. And I remember being happy enough there that as my anxiety would worsen throughout my childhood, one of the few ways my mother could get me to calm down was to have me think about Orlando and to reassure me that we'd go back there someday.

While this particular matter is up in the air under the second Trump administration, one of the easiest ways to legally live in America for at least a year is to be a recent Irish college graduate, and thus be eligible for the J1 visa. The J1 permits you to work in the US for a year if you've graduated in the previous twelve months, or for three months if you are currently in matriculation. If you try to read about Ireland's relationship with the J1 visa online, you will find several sources that describe the programme as a 'rite of passage' for young Irish people. This is not really true. Those who live in America for between three and twelve months on the J1 visa number roughly 3,000 to 5,000 (or less than 0.1 per cent of the population) each year.

Undoubtedly, the J1 visa has an outsized cultural imprint. In the late 2000s, there was an entire genre of Irish music that seemed to be rather nakedly predicated on having spent your summer in the United States. The Coronas, in between touring every private school on the southside of Dublin to do lunchtime gigs, had a hit with 'San Diego Song', while The Thrills scored the biggest hit of their career with a track called 'Big Sur', referring to the mountainous area on California's central coast. The Script's highly Americanised sound could probably be attributed to the fact that they'd been living and working as musicians in Los Angeles for years before they ever became famous. Maybe it was a little weird that so many of our rock bands were playing songs about what it was like to spend your summer in California before dutifully returning to your Business and Economics course in UCD or your graduate job at Anglo-Irish Bank, but it was a marked step forward from changing our names at Ellis Island before rising the ranks to become the most brutal cops the streets of New York, Boston and Chicago had ever seen and pulling up the ladder behind us. Nevertheless, the fact remains that the overwhelming majority of Irish people do not emigrate to America for any amount of time, and thus the J1 visa is not a rite of passage for anyone besides people who want to be able to talk (or, in some cases, sing) about having lived in America, whenever the subject of America comes up, for the rest of their lives.

A J1 is not cheap, either. Between the price of the visa itself, the mandatory health insurance, and having at least a little money in your bank account flying over, the cost of the whole thing before you even set foot on American soil – or the liminal grey area that is US preclearance in the basement of Dublin Airport – came to about €7,000 for me. Apparently, having five grand in your bank account is, or at least was, enough to convince the US State Department that you're not there to rob the gaff. *Illegally work for tips? Moi? With a net worth of roughly three thousand dollars after paying off my first and last month's rent plus a security deposit? I think you've got the wrong guy.*

The grad visa does come with conditions, you see, chief among them that you're not supposed to take work in the service industry. The grad visa only entitles you to work internships, lest you take a job away from a hard-working American. The contradiction, of course, is that internships – neither in America nor anywhere else on earth that I know of – don't pay properly, so the most obvious solution is to do both, and to do your bar work off the books. The best-case scenario is to pick up a job in an Irish bar where the owner knows the score, somewhere near Times Square or Broadway, where some J1-ers become rich beyond their wildest dreams (as long as their wildest dreams clock in at somewhere in the region of, once again, a few thousand dollars).

I was fortunate to fly over at the same time as several of my friends from college, though I hadn't really planned it that way. I'd have been going even if nobody else was. By early 2016, which was when I began the application process, I was mired in the expectation of some unnamed doom, paranoid and unstable, feeling like I wasn't much longer for this earth. At that time, moving to New York felt like the furthest thing from giving up, and a reasonable way to bet on my own salvation. New York, after all, has a reputation for changing lives. My life needed changing and, having turned twenty-three, I figured I'd breeze through JFK with my suitcase and tear through the Big Apple like Thoroughly Modern Millie and make Something of myself.

Believe it or not, my plan had been to work in sales — something a friend of mine who shared my hitherto slacker sensibilities had managed to pull off. Apparently one short year working in the Irish media was enough to make me want to sell out completely and trade in my aspirations as a writer to be a guy who sold things. Didn't especially matter what or to whom. I'd probably have drawn the line at weapons, but who's to say? That's all hindsight. As it turns out, when you interview for a sales position, the people interviewing you can actually tell that you don't know or care about sales. I had one friendly conversation in the offices of NewsWhip, in a Wall Street skyscraper, with an Irish guy who had very impressively climbed the ladder there, and when I told him I was trying to pivot from multimedia journalism to sales, he looked at me with four-parts derision and one-part sympathy, and I realised how clueless and arrogant I'd been to think there was anything that qualified me to tell people what they should buy and why. Still, I can't help but feel my potential was underestimated. Sure, these days I can't make a phone call without suppressing the urge to apologise to whomever I've called for interrupting their day, and indeed for being alive in the first place, but maybe if I'd started at twenty-three I'd be a master by now.

Me and my pal Dee had made a plan to live together, though we knew we'd need a third to bring our rent down to a manageable level. Thankfully, Dee found someone who'd been in her French class to complete our household, sparing us the indignity, nay, insanity, of making an American friend, which is not really the done thing on the J1. You move to the greatest melting pot on earth and you return home with thirty new Irish friends. That's how it works.

Dee and I stayed in an Airbnb just up from the Myrtle–Wyckoff subway station for our first ten days in the city.

Diligent organiser that she is, Dee had ascertained that it wouldn't take us more than a week and a half to pick up an apartment in New York, and so it proved. New York City in 2016 remains the only experience of my life as a renter where apartment supply actually met demand. Dee and I did a full tour of Ridgewood – Palmetto, Woodbine, Seneca, Onderdonk – viewing at least a dozen apartments, each of them perceptibly old, scratch marks on their softwood floors, busted front-door buzzers, all of them with just about enough room to spread your arms widthways. We'd have been thrilled with any of them. Something about those first few weeks in New York turned me into a yokel, smiling like a labrador at the way brokers and estate agents would specify the intersection of streets and avenues. 'Oh, that's at the corner of Bleecker and Seneca.' I can still imagine myself nudging Dee with my elbow: *Did you hear that? Bleecker* and *Seneca. Only in New York!*

Shortly after getting my phone unlocked, something I'd forgotten to do before flying out, I called my mother to see how she was doing, and I'd never heard her voice like I heard it then.

Because my phone had been out of action, it had been maybe three or four days since we'd last spoken, which at that point was a record for us. When she answered, she sounded like she was taking her first breath after a coma, like she'd been expecting never to hear from me again. She asked me where I was and I told her I was at the Myrtle–Wyckoff train station, heading for 14th Street Union Square, and it made me feel like the main character in any of the innumerable songs about how New York was a hell of a town and that if you can make it there you can supposedly make it anywhere. Granted, a lot of those songs seem to come from a time when New York was primarily occupied by gangsters, unscrupulous talent agents and hot-dog vendors rather than yuppies, more yuppies, international yuppies and a waning handful of real people.

In the meantime, the rest of the world had become a more cutthroat place, too. You didn't need to move to New York to get your dreams crushed and your heart turned to stone. A more fitting sentiment for the modern age would be 'if you can make it anywhere, you should thank your lucky stars and stay very still but, at the time, it felt like even saying the names of the stations I was travelling between was an achievement that sufficiently proved my worth in this world. If a platform pusher had got me right there and then, I probably would have gone out happy.

There was no grand plan as to how being in New York would meaningfully improve my life. There were brief moments when I contemplated going to some improv classes at the Upright Citizens Brigade and inevitably becoming a famous actor or comedian, like every sitcom actor or late-night host whose Wikipedia page I'd ever read. I thought about the prospect of finding an American wife who would give me leave to stay for long enough that my as yet unbegun career in comedy or writing or music (or any number of the arts that I'd convinced myself I could be proficient in) could really take off.

Still, leaning over that platform, staring down at the collection of dollar-slice pizza places, liquor stores and bodegas, their 1990s awnings and signage, feeling the cool, dry October breeze, I remember how happy I felt in that moment that – if nothing else – at least it looked like I was doing something. I had spent months saving my money, stomached going to the US embassy for my interview – where I waited in line behind a guy whose bid to return to the US to see his wife and child was savagely rejected because he'd overstayed his visa last time around to marry the poor woman – and quit a job in digital journalism where I'd been steadily proving myself a semi-competent employee for the previous year and a half. Until that point, it had mostly been a lifetime wherein my mistakes often seemed to make more sense than the things I did on purpose. At the time, I thought my mother had just been relieved to hear my voice. It occurs to me now that there may have been more to it.

Irish 'Mammy' humour has always jarred with me – the whole thing of wooden-spoon warnings, the obsession to the exclusion of all else with drying and the immersion, and the suggestion that flat commonalities like these, dictated as they are by the structure of society and traditions dating back decades, are in some way necessary elements of Irish motherhood. Maybe some Irish mothers enjoy the caricature, but I have always been keenly aware that my own mother would not – indeed, it would grieve her even to learn that there is such a bulky catalogue of online humour based on the Frickerisation of Irish mothers.

My mother was born in her own grandmother's home on the Glenealy Road in 1960 and raised in a Crumlin council house, six kids living in two bedrooms. Had there been any money for her to go to university, I suspect that she would have made an unimpeachably talented solicitor or barrister or whatever it was that she'd have enjoyed doing. Even knowing this, I fear that my own understanding of my mother is often oversimplified, that I still see her too much through the lens of having been dependent on her for so long, and being unable to separate her role as my mother from her personhood.

At the time of that phone call from New York, I assumed there could be nothing better for my mother than to hear her eldest son's voice after a few days of radio silence. Like she had nothing else to be living for. Maybe she wasn't relieved for her own sake. Maybe she was relieved for me. Maybe she was thinking, *There, now, maybe he's finally beginning to figure it out.* She had always been the type to stay up until all hours to make sure I came home safely from a night out. Every girlfriend I've ever had has made fun of me for how many texts I get from my mother. She would have wanted more than anything for me to love New York, for me to finally be able to appreciate this fun, frivolous life that she'd so sacrificed so much to provide.

Besides any plans to somehow get a script I'd never written in front of a HBO executive I'd never meet, I think I just wanted to be able to tell my mother I was happy, that I'd made the right choice for once in my life and that it was paying off. That I was fulfilled. Standing on that subway platform waiting for the L train, I think I was able to do that. It didn't last, such things never do, but it was worth it to hear my mother sound relieved and happy for me, if only for a time.

Eventually, Dee and I settled on an apartment around the corner from where four of our close friends had found a sublet. One block over and four blocks down – the kind of thing you don't get to say in Dublin, where streets run on and serpentine for so long that they simply change their names every couple of yards. Camden Street, Wexford Street, George's Street. It's all the same street, man.

The morning we met our superintendent Lisa to pick up the keys, she beckoned us into the courtyard of this renovated townhouse, which had been split into five or six apartments, and looked at us conspiratorially.

'They warned you about the neighbour, right?'

Dee and I laughed, assuming that this was just an example of classic superintendent humour. Our assumption would prove to be incorrect.

'He's a little crazy,' Lisa told us, keeping her voice cheerful and chirpy even as a sombre gravity began to cloud her eyes, and while her language may have been indelicate, she was also massively underselling the situation. When we asked her to elaborate further, she seemed to realise that she might be about to blow a sale and desperately tried to conceal her original meaning. 'No, no. It's just that he's friendly. He's just a bit too friendly.'

Before we'd even furnished the apartment with as much IKEA flatpack as we could afford, including the worst, cheapest couch known to the human ass, it became clear that what Lisa had been trying to say was that our neighbour appeared to be suffering from violent and disturbing psychosis. His housing situation was unstable. At different times his apartment seemed also to be occupied by his mother, or a young woman with a child whose connections to the man were unclear. The man appeared to experience regular bouts of intense distress, spending hours idly banging on our shared walls, blaring heavy-metal music at 4 a.m., screaming matches wherein he accused his cohabitants of having poisoned him, all behind walls that afforded him no privacy. You don't need to spend an entire year in New York City to realise that the state – and perhaps the country at large – does little to take care of its poor, mentally-ill population. A long walk through Midtown is enough to tell you that.

While I managed to avoid most of these episodes by having fortuitously chosen the room furthest from the shared wall, I did overhear him one night in the streets just below my window, chanting 'Heil Hitler'. Every now and then, we'd listen as Child Protective Services turned up to his door, a situation that only ever got as far as a tug of war through those paper-thin walls. We explored our options as to whether there was any kind of care that could be provided to this man, and it became clear there was no such outlet (at least, not any that could be trusted).

We'd moved into that place on the first of November, precisely one week before Donald Trump was elected president for the first time. I had flown out of Dublin airport just a couple of weeks after the Access Hollywood tape had come out, the one with the 'grab them by the pussy' audio. For a few weeks, it seemed like that actually mattered to people. I know, as recently as 2016 we were all stupid enough to think that an admission of such grievous sexual misconduct was like ... important. In the immediate aftermath of the tape coming out, all of Trump's 'surrogates' – a word we all became way too comfortable using in that context, by the way – seemed to abandon him. Even Mike Pence, the bloodless thunderbird puppet Trump had chosen for his vice-president, made for the hills and cancelled his various campaign appearances.

By the morning of election day, the overwhelming majority of commentators and analysts had long since deemed the election to be a foregone conclusion. *The New York Times* 'Needle' gave Hillary Clinton a 99 per cent chance of winning the White House. Indeed, to think that Trump stood a chance of victory showed a lack of sophistication, a dereliction in your duty to spend time reading sites like FiveThirtyEight and Vox, all of which repeated comforting analyses that leaned hard on the unprecedentedness of everything about Donald Trump's campaign, the crude mocking of the disabled reporter who had criticised him, his targeting of military veterans who had grazed as sacred cows for so long in the American mindset, his seeming aversion to everyone else in his party. In hindsight, one understands that it was the unprecedentedness that had buoyed him and worked in his favour all along, and while some people were smart enough to figure that out at the time, I wasn't one of them.

On the day of the election, two of my friends from college and I – two of us on a J1 grad visa for the year and a third on an ESTA before flying home in January to take up a job in finance – wandered around New York City, leaving our apartments in Ridgewood and heading as far as the Javits Center over on 11th Avenue, where the Clinton victory party was set to be held. There was very little to see though; as we made our way back into Midtown we passed dozens of women ready to celebrate the first woman president, many of whom were dressed in suffragette garb like Emmeline Pankhurst, holding up signs bearing slogans like: *This pussy grabs back.* A week earlier, the same two guys and I had run into Ruairí, an old school friend of mine, in a McDonald's on 3rd Avenue. Ruairí had been working in Manhattan for a few years, also in a finance job, and when he told me he thought

Trump was going to win, I dismissed him as a dilettante. *I bet this guy doesn't even read* Politico. But Ruairí was sure, and he made me look a fool. My friends and I arrived at a bar in Bushwick on election night just as Ohio had as good as been called for Trump and an assortment of Brooklynites were already crying on the footpath outside. And for the next few hours, enormous wall-mounted screens played out what felt like the end of civilisation, swing state after swing state going red. My friend Mark, who was coming towards the end of his year-long grad visa at the time, put his arm around my shoulder.

'Don't worry, man,' he said. 'It's just the end of the world.'

It did feel like the end of the world, then. It seemed a certainty that a Trump presidency would accelerate the chaos that had already begun to engulf the Western world in the wake of Brexit. Much like Brexit, Donald Trump's ascension seemed to affirm a new reality in which enormous swathes of the population appeared either unable to distinguish between truth and lies or simply didn't care. In 2016, the rift that had emerged between truth and public perception was still shocking, still felt like an aberration, like something that would be reversed once its consequences were borne out in full. Instead, we should have seen it for what it was – a nigh-inevitable next step for an economic system that had spent the previous several decades obliterating the planet's climate defences, devaluing labour until price increases dwarfed wage increases, and a political facade that shunts the blame for these crimes onto whatever vulnerable cohort the public seems most apt to blame.

At that time, a core plank of Donald Trump's platform was his promise to ban travel from several majority-Muslim countries. This was something he dutifully enacted shortly after his inauguration, the one his administration infamously and falsely claimed had 'the largest audience ever to witness an inauguration – period – both in person and around the globe'. Across social media, well-meaning liberals busied themselves by posting side-by-side shots of Trump's comparatively paltry crowd and better attended events, a move about as efficacious as all of the pre-election strategies had been. *Last Week Tonight* host John Oliver, for example, had tried to lead a hashtag campaign of people referring to Trump as 'Drumpf', the hazy rationale behind which involved drawing attention to Trump's own immigrant background. Others, like his own party's Marco Rubio, had focused on the size of his hands, while millions globally took issue with his fake tan or his hair or the way he would misspeak about virtually any policy area. None of this made any difference and, if anything, only showed the liberal hand to the right and the alt-right and the far right. It confirmed that there was nothing real in the arsenal, no actual force that would be brought to bear on those gearing up to dismantle the order of things. Donald Trump would continue to course through the global information system like a virus, fostering hate against any person or community from whom he could extract no other use, and feckless liberals would put the word 'covfefe' on a T-shirt and sell it to their followers in the name of #Resistance.

In the context of Trump's Executive Order 13769 – referred to in the media and by Trump himself as the 'Muslim ban' – the J1 visa felt less like a celebration of the special diasporic relationship between Ireland and the US and more like naked white supremacy. The idea that there is something innately safe about Irish people, some automatic kinship between us and this empire nearly 7,000 kilometres away, such that we should be fast-tracked for access to the United States, is an idea that we should be ashamed of rather than embrace fulsomely. On the night the ban was first announced, there were protests across the United States. My friend Mike and I travelled to JFK Airport, the same airport we'd flown into just a few months earlier, to protest outside Arrivals. We were quick to shift to the back of the crowd whenever the NYPD encroached. Brave enough to stand in solidarity with the kind of people who actually pay the price of these fascistic whims, though not brave enough to actually risk our own visas.

During those first three months in New York, I sustained myself on savings and on working freelancing shifts for my old employer. Eventually, I landed an internship whose wages were pegged to the state's minimum wage. I woke up at six every morning to do some reporting for a hip-hop blog that had inexplicably sought to procure my services, and I'd be out the door by 7.45 to get the L train from DeKalb to Union Square where I'd switch for the 4, 5 or 6 to Grand Central Station. (I've always thought that heaven's waiting room must look something like Grand Central Station when it's empty.)

I thought I loved New York until I realised that a rush hour subway car was completely incompatible with my need to not be pressed bodily against another human for an hour on my way to and from work. Even now, I remember the sweat dripping from my nose onto my tie, the sting of melted hair gel dripping into my eyes like tallow. It was something about this specific atmosphere of exposure, the recycled air, the inevitable touching of thighs on those blue plastic benches, the human grease on every subway pole.

I was having increasingly abnormal thoughts about myself and my interactions with others. I began to dread any and every fleeting moment of human contact for fear I would somehow contaminate whoever came into contact with me with diseases I almost certainly did not have in the first place. And I began to spend a lot of my free time indulging in my disordered thinking about the United States' carceral system.

By the end of 2017, 1,489,400 people were incarcerated in US prisons, or 0.45 per cent of the population. Proportionally, this is close to five times as many people as leave Ireland for the US on a J1 visa, in a good year. I began to suffer from bouts of severe paranoia, including sincere beliefs that, for example, the CIA would come crashing through our three-bedroom Ridgewood apartment and disappear me to a black site, where I'd be tortured to death by Tommy Lee Jones from *The Fugitive*. As a result, I began to cause quite serious problems for myself.

Even though I'd now fulfilled the terms of my visa by getting an internship, I found it impossible to send the paperwork through to the organisation that had sponsored me to be in the US in the first place. My worry over the legitimacy of my status in the country – founded on nothing, by the way – had devolved into delusion, and whenever I printed off the paperwork, my eyes would focus on the blank spaces between the black-ink lettering, and the fear that the State Department or whoever would read these files and decipher some code or secret message that would prompt them to come and get me begin to eat my heart. My only solution was to take pictures of the documents and send them to a friend who had studied psychology and, better still, had known me well since we'd been young teenagers. She would verify that the documents looked to her as they did to me, that my eyes were not deceiving me, and that they were safe to send. Even so, it took me months.

Some time in July, a few days before my friends Mike and Lily left the city to each return to a Master's programme, the three of us took a boat out on the Hudson River. *Huh, so that's what New Jersey looks like.* By that point, the pressure had been building in my head for months, my intestines had twisted round themselves a thousand times over. I never like to say that I was 'spiralling', because it's never felt that way. It felt, instead, like an endless headlong plummet in the direction of the concrete.

Our boat trip was ostensibly a day out to celebrate the time Lily and Mike had spent in New York but, at some point in the middle of what was probably a very a pleasant conversation, I took a wild stab and said something like, 'I think I need to start taking better care of myself', and promptly burst into tears. In what was probably one of my last opportunities to explain to other people what was happening to me, I did what I could to explain what was going through my mind: my fears of being surveilled, my growing mistrust of technology. From Mike and Lily's perspective it must have been like sitting on a boat with the Unabomber as he wept in their arms. They were seemingly unperturbed that I had made their day all about me, and spent an obscene amount of time being the first people in my life to let me sit with them and simply list my intrusive thoughts and then reassure me that they weren't true.

'You don't think the CIA are watching me?'

'Nope.'

'And you don't think I killed someone on the subway over here and then forgot about it?'

'Probably not, buddy.'

I don't know what would have happened to me if I hadn't started crying in front of them that day. Or if, instead of showing me patience and understanding, they had looked askance at my bewildered rambling. It is within these fine margins that the people we love save our lives.

The conversation didn't make me any more sane, but it did just enough to make life bearable again. I began to rely on the pair of them heavily for reassurance when I was worried about some off-the-wall happenstance, and their stabilising influence did just enough for me redouble my efforts at making something of my time in the US. With around four months to go until my visa was up, I decided to see the country beyond New York City and Orlando, Florida.

Shortly after my trip on the boat, I sat down and made a passable itinerary, figuring out a route that seemed to more or less make sense in that all of the destinations were pretty much one after the other going downward before swinging up left and through Texas. I'd be stopping in Knoxville, Asheville, Charleston, Birmingham, New Orleans and Houston. Fantasist that I was, I harboured some intention of eventually making it as far west as Yellowstone. God only knows how I thought that was going to work. A lifetime spent assuming that things will go wrong has left me poorly suited to understanding the mechanics of how things might go right. It is rarely, if ever, that I have any sense of what I am supposed to do in order to bring about the outcome I want. In fact, it strikes me that 'what I want' has probably always been limited by constraints that come with knowing how to do so little – being unable to rent a car, being too scared to fly, not having anywhere near enough money saved up to think about staying anywhere that wasn't a motel on the side of a highway, an Uber's ride away from the downtown. It was an ill-fated idea, but when you know that an idea is ill-fated ahead of time, you can take steps to manage your own expectations, and ultimately revel in your own failure. Years later, Lily would tell me that Mike had been very worried that I was going to die on that trip.

I was mugged within ten minutes of getting off the Greyhound bus in Knoxville, Tennessee. Or at least that feels like the most straightforward way to describe what happened. There are probably philosophical questions to be considered over what constitutes a mugging. If it's as simple as being stuck in a Knoxville bus station after dark, still at least an hour from your final destination of Gatlinburg, when a rake-thin man with a ponytail and khaki jacket approaches you and tells you he's somehow made his way from Wyoming to Tennessee via Greyhound (a 2,250-kilometre journey that would take about three days to complete, requiring God only knows how many changeovers) and he needed $20 in the dead of night, in the centre of Knoxville, and if that man doesn't take no for an answer when you tell him you have no cash and instead helpfully makes you aware that there's an ATM 'right over there' and then the man accompanies you to the ATM while you wonder if he's about to see just how much he can take you for, then, yes, it was a mugging. There were mitigating factors, however, the primary one being that who knows what would have happened had I said no. Maybe he'd have relented immediately. It doesn't feel good to judge. But it also doesn't feel good to spend twenty-two hours on a bus from New York's Port Authority all the way to Tennessee after an hour-long stopover in Virginia only to immediately be relieved of $20 through your own stupidity.

In the end, I did the only thing a young man who'd just arrived in late-night Knoxville could do. I went over to the ATM, took out the money and handed it over with a grace that I hoped said 'Thank you for not taking even more of my money' without suggesting I had any more money that he could take. This was more or less exactly what I had expected to happen.

After saying goodbye to Andrew Jackson and the man who had rehoused him, I mercifully found a taxi driver who was prepared to make the hour-long drive out to the foot of the Smoky Mountains. By the time we got to Gatlinburg, the town was shut down. I had known I'd be getting in shortly after midnight, but for whatever reason I'd assumed at the time that I'd be able to brazen it out until dawn, so I wouldn't need accommodation on that first night. Maybe I hadn't been expecting to get out of Knoxville so fast, maybe I'd even been harbouring thoughts of seeing the World's Fair Sunsphere, an 81-metre-tall hexagonal steel truss structure erected to celebrate the 1982 World's Fair (whatever that was), from the episode of *The Simpsons* where Bart gets his driver's licence. It dawned on me rather suddenly that I had neither the money nor the organisational wherewithal to pull this trip off – not even if I stuck to the tight budget I'd vaguely imagined for myself – and that it was entirely possible I would be sleeping on the streets of Gatlinburg until the sun came up.

Even at night, the town twinkled with the kind of unreality so often a feature of towns whose purpose is to provide a service to those who pass through it, rather than somewhere for people to live. Instead of schools, there were trinket shops with racks of T-shirts that told of how great it was to be in the state of Tennessee. They love slogan T-shirts in that part of the world. Despite my assumptions about the conservative nature of Tennessee, one T-shirt replicated in many storefronts read: *I'm not gay, but $20 is $20*, suggesting a progressive attitude towards both sexual orientation and sex work not always associated with the Volunteer State. One more paradoxical T-shirt I spotted bore an enormous star-spangled crucifix and read: *Stand for the flag, kneel for the cross.* My knees locked up just looking at it and I eventually tore myself away from it lest the Sphinx's riddle overcome me entirely. Most of the other T-shirts I could see through the windows carried threats of gun violence – in some cases explicitly, in others just sort of implied:

Gun safety rule #1: Carry one.

No Trespassing: Are you going to listen to me in English or am I going to have to speak to you in 12-gauge?

The average response time of a 911 call is 23 minutes. The average response time of a .357 is 1,400 feet per second.

How anyone could spend a year in the United States and not end up paranoid was beyond me.

After a time spent wandering – and some added time spent sitting, slumped, wondering what exactly it was about me that had prevented me from simply organising any form of shelter for my first night in a strange, new place – I found a motel with a front office that was still open. It was easily 2 a.m. by then, probably later. The girl behind the counter looked at me quizzically and asked if I understood that I'd have to check out in a matter of hours and I said yes, I just needed somewhere to sleep. When I got to my room there was a large and loud bug throwing itself suicidally against the door. If there were any coherent thoughts swimming through my mind in that moment, they would have read something like: *What is this creature? Is this thing why they need the guns? Because if so, I'm starting to get it.*

After slumping against the hallway wall and sliding down onto my arse, practically asleep with my forehead perched precariously on my bundled-up knees, I resolved to overcome this hellspawn. I took off my sweater and shooed it away before getting through the door in enough time to prevent the thing from following me in. I can't remember what I googled in order to identify this abomination. *Enormous, loud, potentially Confederate winged bug*, perhaps. It was a cicada, as it turned out, the closest thing that real world has to a Hieronymus Bosch monster. Nevertheless, I crashed in my room and woke up the next morning and checked out without showering, making straight for the cable car that takes you up over the whole town.

It was an overcast, humid August day and the clouds rested eerily on the mountain range that ringfenced the town. From above, I caught sight of a clapboard wedding chapel, a dozen restaurants, families making their way through the town in matching T-shirts, and a museum complex underneath a large sign that read: 'Christ in the Smokies'. My curiosity piqued, I reminded myself to remain safely within the confines of the cable car until I made it back to terra firma to investigate what exactly Jesus Christ had been up to in the Volunteer State. I love state nicknames, by the way. I think it's the funniest thing in the world for whenever someone tells me they've been to some flyover state, the more anonymous the better, to go, 'Ah yes, West Virginia: The Aloha State.' Nobody finds this as funny as I do.

I guess I must have been trying to save money or something because I can't for the life of me think why I wouldn't have paid the entrance fee into Christ in the Smokies. It's a mystery to me, I've never been that type. I would say being easily parted from my money is one of my most core characteristics. You can get $20 from me just by having a ponytail and bumping into me at a bus station. I just know that I didn't see fit to pay in, and I regret it to this day. Though it's since been demolished, Christ in the Smokies was, for all intents and purposes, a museum dedicated to the life and times of Jesus Christ, sitting at the foot of the Smoky Mountains in Gatlinburg, Tennessee. I did step into the foyer and take a long, hard look inside. When I strain my memory, I can remember a glass case protecting a range of 'artefacts' that, as far as I could tell, was just a community theatre-costume department approximation of the kinds of cloth Jesus might have worn or coins that sort of looked like coins he might have used. I'm pretty sure Christ in the Smokies didn't have the budget to house any of the real shit from Aramaic times. Especially if not even a schmuck like me was paying entry.

What stood out to me more than anything else was one of

those seaside amusement cardboard cutouts – you know, the ones where you put your face in a round hole and it looks like you've got the body of a Viking or a cow or the Dalai Lama. This place had one of those, except the hole you could put your face in belonged to the body of a Roman guard who was apprehending Jesus. Sort of seems like that's the last person any God-fearing Christian would want to be in that situation, but okay. At least Judas and Pontius Pilate had some characterisation.

I spent two full days in Gatlinburg, wandering through the Great Smoky Mountains National Park and listening to 'Wichita Lineman' on repeat because Glen Campbell had just died. There were signs all over the park warning visitors not to get any closer than 50 feet to a bear, which I always enjoyed because, if I'm 50 feet from a bear, whether or not that distance narrows is going to be entirely up to the bear. After about two hours of walking and the realisation – which I had failed to pre-emptively google – that the park was 522,427 acres in size, I decided to make the two-hour trek back to town. It was rapidly becoming clear to me that you can travel the South without much money, and you can travel the South without doing any planning, but you can't really do both at once.

That evening I stopped into a large moonshine emporium – the Ole Smoky Distillery – closer in aesthetic to a Body

Shop than an off-licence. They were using the word 'moonshine' but it wasn't like some drifter selling moonshine out of a train car. Though that would have been cool. No, it was an enormous glossy operation, where I paid tax at the till and got a receipt for my two 70cl shoulders of the strongest moonshine I could find. It seemed like a fitting souvenir from that part of the world, and I stuffed the bottles into the bottom of my travel backpack, underneath layers of clothes and towels and whatever electronics I could carry.

On my last day before moving on from Tennessee to North Carolina, I decided I would calm my nerves with a trip to Dollywood: the Dolly Parton-themed theme park. Parton had long been a hero of mine, since the first time I heard 'Jolene' on the cassette tape of country classics my father would play in the car whenever we drove down to see his family in Wexford. It was a stellar playlist – 'Rhinestone Cowboy', 'The Devil Went Down to Georgia', 'Achy Breaky Heart', and a whole bunch of Nanci Griffith, may she rest in peace. This was before the memeification of Dolly Parton had truly taken off in earnest, but even then she was probably regarded at large as one of the most beloved, least polarising people on the planet. She stood for things like giving books to children, choice feminism and being one of the greatest songwriters and performers of her generation.

I was soon to learn, however, that the town built around Ms

Parton's theme park has a sick secret. Since I'd already checked out of my motel and I'd be boarding a fresh Greyhound bus right after my Dollywood visit, I'd been forced to keep my bottles of moonshine in the bottom of my backpack. As I made for the park's security check, I hadn't even been thinking about them. I only really remembered they were there when a short, bald security guard with a small white plaster that didn't fully cover the cut on his cheek curtly asked me to take every item out of the backpack. This instinctively struck me as excessive, though in hindsight one can see why this would be necessary, what with America's ... area-specific problems. When I removed the two bottles and gave a sheepish shrug, the mood soured quickly.

'Sir, you're lucky you're not spending the night in county jail,' he told me in a thick southern accent and without much ceremony. I had only ever dealt with Orlando-grade theme-park staff before. I had never been spoken to this way. My heart was racing in that moment. Was he joking? I've never understood the wink-nudge humour of the man's man over-fifties demographic. I believed I had a trump card, a trump card I may share with you.

And so I stood tall and spoke the words.

'I'm sorry, sir. I am Irish. I have no idea what's going on.'

Naturally, I can't remember exactly how I formulated the phrase, but it was something along the lines of *I am Irish, therefore not only can I not be expected to know the rules, but now that you understand I am Irish, I also expect to be exempted from whatever bullshit rules I didn't learn in the first place, now get out of my fucking way so I can meet Dolly Parton.* For the first time in my life, maybe for the first time in history, it didn't work.

'Son, you're lucky I'm not calling the sheriff right now,' he said, effectively ruling out any double-down I might attempt on the old shamrock card. Not only that, but he was leaning even harder into this whole 'night in the county jail' bit, which, given my paranoid predisposition, was causing me to panic quite badly. What was I to do? What was the protocol for a situation like this? I thought about the kind of people who travel in groups, the kind of people who plan their trips, the kind of people who book their accommodation before they get to Christ in the Smokies and don't develop a mortal distaste for cicadas because they don't like the vibe of the only one they've ever met. How would someone like that get out of this jam? *Do I make a run for it? I don't kill him, do I?*

In that moment, I believe my tongue was a little tied up as my brain tried to process what this man was telling me. It briefly occurred to me to say something clever that would probably make him kick the shit out of me, like, 'On what charges?' or to simply ask him, 'Sir, can you please explain to me why on earth I would be going to jail for inadvertently bringing these bottles of moonshine into Dollywood?'

Those questions seem, in hindsight, pretty reasonable. Instead, I withered under his wraparound sunglasses stare, feeling like Cool Hand Luke under the pitiless gaze of Boss Godfrey, and I told him apologetically that I would get rid of the bottles. He gave me no indication whatsoever that my concession pleased him, which was his right. I had broken the law, apparently, or at least some very strange moral code that this man adhered to. But if you know what kind of man I am, you know I'd never put two bottles of moonshine before a lady, and especially not a lady like Dolly Parton, and besides, I'd already spent $70 on the ticket.

Mooching outside the entrance gates, I was struck by a moment of divine inspiration. I hurried over to the lost-and-found kiosk and held up a bottle in each hand like I was trying to get the party started in a 2000s music video. I asked the woman behind the counter if she could just sort of, you know, pretend that I lost the bottles, before reclaiming them at the end of the day. The old lost-and-found con. The woman behind the counter, old and small, took one of the bottles from me and examined it before telling me she couldn't be liable for it.

I nodded, though I didn't really understand. *Liable? County jail? Sheriff's office? Why do these people keep saying these things?* After spending ten months in New York, the last six of which had been taken up mostly with freaking out about the consequences of sending mail or touching off the poles on the subway, was I about to be brought down on bootlegging charges?

I sat forlornly on the kerb until the back of my neck started to burn, wondering if there was any obvious place I could stash my moonshine. Holding on to the drink had stopped seeming worth it quite a while ago. I cut my losses and placed both bottles carefully in a bin, and while I had no real intention of fishing them back out later on, I did take a mental note of where the bin was just in case I changed my mind.

In a show of goodwill, I returned to the security queue and made sure I was in the same line again, so I could repair my relationship with the man who'd threatened to turn me in mere moments earlier. When I got to the front, I smiled like a coward, saying, 'I got rid of the bottles' and stood there like I was waiting for a hug from a father who hated me.

His mood did not soften.

'You better have,' he told me, and he watched on, impassive as the sun, while I took everything I'd brought south with me out of my backpack yet again. He said nothing this time, so I said, 'I can go in?'

He nodded yes, though at the time I couldn't help but wonder if it was some kind of ploy on his part. Now, he knew exactly where I was. Now, when the cops showed up it would be like shooting fish in a barrel.

As I entered the park, I called my mother to explain the situation. She wasn't relieved to hear my voice this time.

I think that, up until that point, I had done a relatively good job of concealing my precipitous decline from her. By now, I was unable to plug my laptop into hotel sockets to charge for fear my thoughts would be read, my private conversations leaked, my innermost secrets used against me somehow. Staring at any one thing or any one person for too long triggered waves of deep paranoia. I would hold receipts in my hand for hours, unable to let go of anything that had touched my person. Before I checked out of any accommodation I would take videos, dozens of minutes long, in which I would record every nook and cranny of the room in case I'd left anything behind.

I have always been impressed by how well my mother listens to me talk about things that aren't actually a big deal as if they are about to cause my sudden and total destruction, if not the destruction of our family and the world at large. In all my years of freaking out over imaginary medical issues, non-existent threats to my person, the fears that I have contaminated others with diseases I don't have, she has never once said, 'Oh no, what are we going to do?' She has never once wavered. She knows I'm not quite right, and she's smart enough to never be taken in by the same fears that consume me.

She was patient as ever in listening to me spell out my delusion that I was about to be lifted off the streets of Tennessee and God only knew what would happen after that. Gently, she suggested that maybe my mind wouldn't go to such places if I didn't insist on travelling alone. Constructive. Boring. Correct. Unhelpful. I thanked her for her counsel and when I hung up I stayed on my phone to google what the story was with moonshine in Tennessee. Is moonshine illegal in …? Is liquor illegal in …? As it turned out, when I had taken the trolley from Gatlinburg to Pigeon Forge, I had crossed from a normal town into a dry town. Indeed, I found out that Tennessee as a state is dry by default, and that its municipalities have to opt out. Technically, Sevier County, where Pigeon Forge (and Dollywood) is, is what's legally known as a 'moist county'. You can get beer at the store and bring it home, and you might, if you're lucky, be able to get spirits at a restaurant, but probably not.

There was nothing to suggest that I'd be clapped in ankle-irons for being in possession of the liquor, so I came to the conclusion that the security guard with the cut on his face had been trying to scare me, but the joke was on him – I was already scared.

As I wandered the park, I let the incongruent unreality sync up before me, the sun putting new freckles on my arms.

It may suggest a rather deep sickness of the soul, but I feel at home in the opiate and saccharine safety of a theme park.

From the corner of my eye, I saw a band of stage performers dressed like The Lumineers playing banjos and doing some kind of do-si-do move in front of a crowd of pleased elderly onlookers. A distant scream emanated from some unseen rollercoaster. Walking there, I noticed a family of many children, all with matching blue shirts and bowl haircuts and I assumed this was some sort of religious sect or social subset that I wasn't familiar with. Nobody else seemed to be staring. Between me and them was another man, with his back to me, wearing a T-shirt emblazoned with the slogan: *Tennessee moonshine! It's only illegal if you get caught*. I wondered about my moonshine in the bin outside, whether it was still there.

This, all of this, was the reason I'd come to Tennessee, I told myself. Whether or not it lived up to my expectations was beside the point. I thought about how my mother had sounded when she'd answered the phone that first time I'd called her from Myrtle–Wyckoff. Proud, maybe.

The familiar smell of benzene rose from the asphalt and I breathed it in and thought I'd better try to remember this. Then I made my way to the lockers to get the straps of my recently lightened backpack off my sunburned shoulders for a while.

A Big Thing Of Water

'HOW TO SAVE a Life' by The Fray is a radio-friendly rock song that tells the story of someone who has failed to prevent a friend from sliding into self-destruction. The song's music video is like something a transition-year psychology class might put together as a fundraiser for Pieta House. It features the band playing in a white void in between shots of ordinary human beings staring down the camera, exhibiting a range of poses and expressions – mournful, overjoyed, relieved, tearful – while handy, numbered 'How to Save a Life'-style tips flash on the screen: 18. Talk to Someone. 45. Touch. 22. Cry. 7. Forgive. 99. Say goodbye.

The song was perhaps one of the first pieces of mainstream modern media that was forthrightly concerned with what, in the years that followed, would take shape as the idea of 'mental health', particularly the heavily commercialised idea of mental health that can be maintained by things like chatting with your friends and staying up all night. The version of mental health that even the most wary corporations can get behind. Don't worry, though. This is not an essay about mental health.

The song became a bit of a phenomenon. Shortly after its release, 'How to Save a Life' was used in the popular 2000s medical sitcom *Scrubs*, playing over a scene in which the hitherto infallible tough-guy mentor Dr Cox loses three patients having prematurely actioned three organ transplants from a woman who turned out to have rabies.

The song plays as Cox valiantly and vainly fails to save three lives, and the show's protagonist J.D. watches his mentor fall from his pedestal in real time. The song also featured in other weekday-evening melodramas such as *Grey's Anatomy* and *One Tree Hill*, in scenes I'm prepared to blindly wager also feature people dying. Intuitively, it feels like it should be against the rules for more than one concurrently broadcasting show to use the same song for essentially the same purpose. Such was the chokehold

'How to Save a Life' had on popular culture in the mid-2000s.

It was the early autumn of 2018 and the five of us met on the side of the road opposite the Tallaght Hospital Luas stop and packed ourselves into Johnny's old maroon Ford Focus. I ended up in the middle seat either as a gesture of goodwill or because, at 5 feet 7½ inches, I am the most compact member of The Lads™.

Weeks earlier, in a burst of efficiency that would never be repeated, the idea of a surfing holiday had been suggested, researched and booked over the course of an hour in a Messenger group chat that had existed since the previous year, populated by the Dublin remnants of the friends I'd had in college, those of us left laying on the battlefield after our comrades had made for the Valhalla of emigration. In the meantime we – myself, Johnny, Jamie, Cormac and Conor – had become The Lads™. At the time of writing, I am the only member of the five who still lives in Ireland – and even I've moved away and back twice in the meantime. We'd set up a group chat on Facebook the autumn before to organise a trip to the pub to watch Ireland get smoked 5–1 by Denmark. Soon after we'd gone bowling in

Stillorgan and spent the night bouncing one of the gumball machine balls around a car park until a security guard told us to fuck off and we got a taxi into town and went to Whelan's.

We were a uniformly dorky bunch. To give you an indication of just how unladlike this crew is, the topic of who of was the biggest 'lad' once came up and it was broadly agreed that it was *me*. Me, with my DNA closer to that of a first-draft Jim Henson Muppet than anything approximating a 'real man'. We weren't lads. We were The Lads™.

We'd settled on Lahinch, County Clare, for our trip, a town about which I knew very little at the time. I had never been surfing, I knew I'd be bad at it, but I'd longed all my life to legitimately say something like 'Cowabunga' or 'Radical' and this seemed like a step in the right direction.

To set the mood as we made our way west, Conor hooked up his phone to a Bluetooth speaker and began to play 'The Boys Are Back in Town' by Thin Lizzy. Or at least that's what I thought for about eight minutes until I realised we were listening to the audio of a YouTube video titled something like 'The Boys Are Back in Town But It's Just the Intro on Repeat for Ten Hours'.

The next item on this already strange playlist was a viral

WhatsApp voice note that had been doing the rounds that summer, the kind of voice note you can only stomach if you assume from the get-go that at least 90 per cent of it is bullshit.

The narrator was a young man, posh, with an accent that had evolved beyond the typical hallmarks of D4 Montrose mid-Atlanticism and had become something even more aggressive. You know those guys whose voices are so posh it almost sounds like their larynx is trying to choke the words before they make it out of their mouth? One of those guys.

While the details of the voice note are too inflammatory to reprint in full, as well as profoundly unverifiable, I will say enough about it that you will at least know whether or not you've heard it before. The voice note told the story of students from a private school in Dublin on some kind of missionary trip in Africa, specifically the story of how one of the students on the trip – who apparently had an unspecified learning difficulty – ended up having unprotected sex with a woman from the local area, and the supposed misfortunes thereafter described in gleeful and violent detail. The story climaxes with a teacher supposedly learning of the incident and immediately vomiting everywhere. I had been working in news at the time and never saw even the slightest suggestion that any school in Dublin was working to deal with or address or cover up this incident, and it strikes me as entirely plausible that none of it ever happened.

The five of us sat in horror as the voice note unfolded, and when it was over we focused mostly on debating its veracity, which is a more comfortable conversation to have than: 'What on earth would possess this young man to tell this story, in this way?' We were young men ourselves, and young men don't like to talk about the motivations of other young men.

It was our first trip away together as The Lads™. (I feel compelled to clarify that we don't use the obnoxious little ™ in our communications with each other. That's purely something I am doing for this essay and I am rapidly losing faith in it.)

On our way to Lahinch, we spent at least an hour of sojourn in Obama Plaza, posing with the bronze statues of Barack and Michelle, eating garlic chips from the Supermac's and fruitlessly spending all of the coins we had on a claw machine trying to win a plushy Super Mario or some such. We set off again at around 4 p.m. and, as the overcastness of the day made for a dark evening, Conor piped up to mention that if we didn't get there by six we wouldn't be able to check in. We'd spent too much time and money on the claw machine trying to win those toys. Classic 'lad' behaviour.

We made it in time all the same, set our things down and examined the accommodation. Two rooms with two single beds each and one master bedroom, to be occupied by Johnny as a reward for driving us down. We decided who would room with whom – a ritual I have always found strangely intimate, like a sort of confession. Is it a question of which of our friends we love the most? Who we trust the most? At the risk of generalising, I believe that most men in that situation will tell you they don't have a preference, and maybe some of them mean it. Affecting an air of having no preference is a posture that requires practice, and its evolutionary purpose is unclear. What did nonchalance do for the neanderthals when they were being chased by sabre-tooth tigers? What does it do for us now? In the end, Jamie and I threw our bags down onto two parallel single beds. Partnered for the duration of the trip. In situations like this, 'partnered' is a word that you should only think, never speak aloud. And so we headed off to find a pub.

The young man playing his guitar in the corner seemed to be more or less our age, and talented. He'd been playing trad songs all night, it seemed. It was that kind of pub. Brass lamps, revolutionaries and old alcohol memorabilia on the walls. Do you know the difference between a traditional Irish pub and a traditional English pub? English pubs are like open-plan offices, tables laid out across the floor, evenly spaced, perfect for keeping an eye on everyone while they play bingo. Traditional Irish pubs are more labyrinthine. Snugs, drinkers hidden huddled behind corners, ledges jutting out of big thick load-bearing pillars, steps and mezzanines, and nooks and crannies perfect for planning a rising.

There were four of us sat around the table. Cormac had stayed back at the accommodation working on a job application that, a few months later, would take him out of Dublin for the next seven years and counting. I nursed a pint of Guinness which tasted like every other pint of Guinness I've ever panic-ordered when I end up in a bar that doesn't serve ginger beer. Ginger beer was my thing then, ginger beer or Kopparberg Mixed Fruits. You know, wuss drinks. Anything sweet enough to make the joints in my shoulders hurt if I drank enough of it. I've matured since – now I struggle to drink anything that isn't a pina colada. Guinness, however, has grown to dominate the panic order market.

(I have a theory about how Guinness became so popular, by the way, and it's not about 'splitting the G' or the fact that they can print your face on the head of a pint when you do a tour of the Storehouse. It's because of Instagram, and the fact that Guinness is one of the only photogenic beers in existence. If you know your night out is going to be immortalised on the grid, would you rather be holding something solid black and creamy white or a sloshing glass of piss?)

As the evening grew late and the kitchen closed, the door was eventually darkened by at least a dozen young men, young enough that I would perhaps have described them as 'boys' but for the sheer size of each of them without exception. The boys gave the impression of an all-conquering local sports team, the pride of the village, county champions of this or that. At first, I assumed our evening had been interrupted by the fresh young princes of Lahinch, until one of my own cohort spoke up. 'I recognise some of those guys. I think they were a few years behind me in school.'

These boys didn't all look the same, but there were what one would call 'commonalities'. You could tell that not one of them weighed any less than 90 kilograms, and it would have been almost entirely muscle. There was no outlier, no token dweeb, no speccy little 1980s high-school movie geek following them around with an RC car remote control coming up with hare-brained schemes for how to get into mischief. These guys were jocks. We might have been The Lads™, but these guys were lads for real – lad as in UniLad, LadBible, the kind of guys Danny Dyer could admire.

While they might not have been the celebrated sons of the village, they quite quickly seized control of the pub. They must have been in town longer than we'd been because, within minutes of arriving, they were stood over an older gentleman, encouraging him to drink the shots that had been laid out before him. By that point, me and my crew were still trying to figure out who these guys were, their place in the town. How was it that they had so quickly commandeered the entire building? How come it hadn't occurred to us to do the same? Granted there were fewer of us in number, and there was less of us in sheer body mass, but we were smart guys. Surely, if we'd put our heads together, we could have finagled it so that we were the ones forcing an old man to drink shots for our amusement.

I'm not sure how far into the song he was before we clocked that the guitarist had swung hard out of his own trad playlist and was now playing 'How To Save a Life', apparently at the behest of the pub's new guests. There were enough of the boys to line out at Donnybrook, and every ounce of pressure they could generate between them was being brought to bear on the creaking floorboards of this Lahinch pub. This wood that had been soaking up alcohol for decades no doubt was now enduring the weight of over a dozen fully grown men, bouncing and heaving to the syncopation of The Fray frontman Isaac Slade's chorus.

In a phenomenon that you have likely experienced before, the collective timbre somehow lost its Irishness as the voices rose and converged. Instead, the song took on the characteristics of an English football chant. Sung in the same accent that you might hear 'Football's coming home' or that song about vindaloo by Lily Allen's dad and the floppiest one out of Blur. This impulse to parrot English football and rugby chants in English accents seems to be one of the harder-to-shake colonial legacies, though I had never seen it applied to such a song. These guys were punching the pub's low ceiling, some of them had their arms around each other like they'd just won a cup game.

The air was humid with sweat all of a sudden. Imagine the thumping on the walls and the floor and the ceiling all in tempo with the song's four-four time signature, this weedy little trad singer who, just minutes earlier, had been having another easy night by the fire with a smattering of American tourists and us, just some dorks who barely had the confidence to request a song between them. It seemed that without word or gesture, a bloodless coup had taken place in that pub, and now we were all wrapped up in the anthems of these young men. From the days of Gregorian monks to the most poorly attended local amateur-sporting event of the weekend, the boys have always loved a chant.

At first, there was a raucous delight in watching the American tourists try to figure out what was going on, watching them run the same calculations that I had already been through myself: *I guess these are the local sporting heroes?* Wrong, my friend, I'm pretty sure that these guys went to a private school in Dublin.

As the cluster of boys began to break apart and set up satellites across the bar, a few parenthetical scenes unfolded. My eyes were drawn to one corner in which a man who, if he resembled any celebrity it was a young Woody Allen, sat stone-faced with his beautiful wife, his wife who happened to be engaged in conversation with two of the rowdy boys. They spoke to her as if her partner was not even there, and he seethed visibly, eventually getting up to go to the bathroom. Big mistake, pal. Even at an across-the-room sort of distance, I could see her affecting a posture of interest and intent listening that came from a place of what might have looked like naivety, but was more likely strategic appeasement.

Eventually, after the boys had wrung every tune they'd asked for out of the poor guitar player, things settled down. But not for long. God only knows how, but it seems that through some kind of osmosis, the rugby lads had learned that it was the birthday of some mid-forties-looking American with a bad haircut who appeared to be in town with three or four others, all about his age. He had an unsuspecting air, a lack of self-preservation that even I – with very few bullying instincts – could sniff out. Call it a sixth sense, but I think some part of me knew what they were about to do to this man. I've been around the block; I went to a rugby school. I know how these things are done. Somehow, they talked him into getting up on a chair. Standing there charmlessly in his button-down shirt, I believe that for one brief and shining moment he probably thought he was king of Ireland. The crowd knew to sing 'Happy Birthday'. I don't know how, I don't think the rugby lads passed out a memo or anything, but the song began to swell as more and more people cottoned on that we were singing for this man up on the chair. *They don't sing for me back home,* he was probably thinking, already fantasising about going back to his buddies and making them jealous. Regaling them with tales of the Emerald Isle, that he'd been treated to a real, traditional Irish birthday. An authentic Irish experience where we lowly spudmen serenaded him as he extended his arms before us like a benevolent regent. By this point, we were maybe halfway through the second line of 'Happy Birthday'.

What happened next can only have taken seconds, though in my memory it feels eternal. This man, helpless fool that he was, made the unconscionable mistake of believing that he was in some way in on the joke. One of many happy participants, rather than the unsuspecting object. But that was neither his last mistake nor his gravest.

Up on the chair, with every eye in the pub drawn to him, the singalong crawl of 'Happy Birthday' entering its second round, he did something that I have in fact seen other men do when they are trying to make themselves look as though they are comfortable with the attention they are receiving. He began, teasingly, to unbutton his shirt. I suspect he pulled this move to give the perception of confidence or good-humoured self-deprecation, or some combination of the two. The first button, gone. The second button, gone. Perhaps he looked out over this small sea of cheering, muscular young men and mistook their gleaming, glinting eyes and their cheers as good-faith encouragement. Ah, my sweet Yankee Doodle, if only it were thus.

His shirt hung open by now, revealing the paunchy belly that was to be expected of this small man who appeared smaller with every passing syllable of the world's most famous song. The enthusiasm for transparency and communication around mental health that had been so fervent throughout this pub only minutes earlier had ebbed, and left behind a cut-throat world where no American man was safe to stand on a chair before a legion of boys hardened in rugby dressing rooms, for whom hazing might as well be a second language.

Where were we in the song when it all started to go wrong? Maybe 'Happy Birthday' had finished, maybe the pub had moved on to the interminable addendum of 'For He's A Jolly Good Fellow' by the time two of the lads flanked the man on the chair and encouraged him to give us a little bit more with his performance. *Sure, you've unbuttoned your shirt, but is that all you've got for us? You want to be a star, don't you? C'mon, pal. The whole pub is watching.*

One of the boys made a reach for his waistband. Jokingly. A joke. A simple joke. What would you do in this situation? You've already made the mistake of getting up on the chair, and the Irish people are still singing to you, so you can't exactly get down or you'll risk their wrath. You don't know the rules, after all, and you haven't been around the Irish for long. You've no idea what happens when they turn on you. Maybe the safest thing to do is to stay on the chair. That's probably what's going through your mind. At the time I thought the man was a moron, 2 feet off the ground and performing for us all, for some reason believing himself to be safe. *Why would anyone ever be so stupid as to believe themselves to be safe?* Now I think that he was probably terrified. Probably had no idea what to do. But of all the things he could have done, I will never understand why he opted for unbuttoning his pants.

Any hope there had been of the sharks swimming on by went out the window the moment the waistband began to peel away. The two rugby guys who flanked him, like attendants to an emperor, assisted and encouraged in this process, and the man's trousers came a little further down.

How many verses of 'Jolly Good Fellow' had we sung by that point? I should be able to remember, because I should be able to remember how the song died in everyone's throat the moment one of the rugby boys decided he'd had enough of the gamesmanship. He grabbed hold of the man's boxer shorts and tried to yank them downwards. The singing and the cheers, even the mean-spirited ones, were cut off with a record-scratch as the scene turned ugly and the birthday boy wrestled to preserve his modesty. He grabbed hold of his boxers and strained to keep them in place – Adam holding on to his fig leaf for dear life. A good old-fashioned jocking.

I'd not borne witness to such a thing for many moons. I was twenty-five years old by then, my days of jocking and being jocked long behind me. I can still remember the first time. It was primary school, I can't have been more than ten years old, standing on the sidelines of a school GAA match when one of my classmates got me. Vaguely humiliating? Yes. Character-building? No, not especially. But the single saving grace of that incident, which could have been 'formative' (the worst thing it's possible for any childhood memory to be, by the way) and was instead relegated to merely 'memorable', was that my boxers remained snugly in place. Even at the very height of the jocking phase of my life, nobody was ever going full-jock. You don't pull a man's boxers down, not in the pub, not in the locker room, not ever.

It was perhaps the highest stakes I've ever seen in any game of tug-of-war. We all saw more skin than we should have, but nothing close to full arse or dick or, indeed, balls. I suspect that if, by some chance, the American ever picked up this book and read his tale back, he might not be comforted by these words: *Don't worry, man, I didn't see your arse or your dick or even your balls.* The unseemly back-and-forth elicited a shapeless sort of 'Oh, no' noise from the crowd. Even the young men who had brought about this state of affairs seemed to disavow the act as soon as it had been attempted. Certainly, there were no cheers. The would-be jocker disappeared into the crowd and the American man sat back down, presumably in the first stages of what has surely been a years-long journey to process whatever the hell happened to him that night.

'I don't think that was right,' Johnny said. Not aggressively, not like he was trying to start anything, not even like he was especially trying to be heard, but he certainly didn't mute his voice either. No response came from the quarters of the burly boys, less rowdy all of a sudden, but then they may not have heard it. Who knows what would have happened if they had. Jockings for all, perhaps.

While Johnny may have been the only person in the pub to have spoken up, there was a definite air that the fun had been spoiled, the joke had been taken too far, that obviously the pub would need to hang up a sign that says 'Strictly no jocking the Yanks' to head off developing a reputation as the Yank-jocking pub (though the more I think about that, the more it sounds like a multimillion-euro idea; God, they'd line up in droves). Everything went quiet after that, so we finished our beers and made the two-minute walk back to our apartment, all of us presumably thinking there but for the grace of God with regard to our own waistbands and underwear.

Back in our room, Jamie and I wondered if the American would go home and try to sell the whole thing as a win. Better than the alternative. To explain to his closest friends and family that his trip to Ireland — maybe his first trip to Ireland, maybe a meaningful trip to Ireland (God, what if he'd been there to scatter his father's ashes or something and ended up getting jocked on his birthday?) — culminated in a humiliation ritual. Stood on a chair in a foreign land, fighting for his life, trying to keep his boxers on in front of a crowd of strangers ironically singing 'Happy Birthday' to him, like a nightmare from a sitcom.

It would be wrong of me to paint this group of young men as representative of men at large or to conflate this incident with the much more pernicious evils that men do. In fact, it doesn't even feel especially appropriate for me to render anything like a full judgement against them. I've certainly seen worse. We've all seen worse.

Earlier that summer, I had joined and quickly left a football team when I discovered the team's group chat was full of racist remarks and unsolicited and especially weird pornography. I should have been brave enough to tell them what I thought about their behaviour, but I wasn't. Maybe that makes me the problem. Truthfully, I just didn't know what to say. I was shocked and disappointed, and ultimately without any meaningful recourse. A group of men all reinforcing each other's behaviours are untroubled by the disapproval of one man. The very fact that you have a problem with what they're doing affirms what they knew all along. That you're not one of them, could never be one of them, and can therefore be discounted.

I'm not a biologist or a behaviourist. I can't give you a comprehensive rundown of the evolutionary reasons why men group together, why they make so much noise, or why they so often single out small, weak, poorly protected people and humiliate them. Is it some fear – conscious or unconscious – the nagging feeling that this world is not and never will be safe, and that your best bet as a strong man is to find other strong men who will support you in the meting out of your strength, whatever form that may take? That would be nice, wouldn't it? If we could tell ourselves that all the men who go through this world tormenting others are doing it because they're the cowards. Like the way your mother tells you that your bully is more scared of you than you are of him before he knocks your teeth out the next morning. I don't buy it. I believe it's the libidinal joy of freely exercising power. The security that comes from a lifetime of knowing that in any given dynamic, you are comfortable with your methods of bringing someone else to do your will.

Does that mean that the men I've been lucky enough to call my friends for the past ten years or so are special? That they're exempt from the pressures and conditions that create these toxic traits in other men? As a man myself, I don't think any of us are exempt from those conditions and every man needs to find his own way to rage against them.

We were only in Lahinch for forty-eight hours, though it felt like longer. We got a lot done on our second day in the town. We went surfing and for some reason I, who had never surfed before, asked the cool surf people in their little seaside surf shack for a hard board instead of a foam board. I don't know why, all I know is I'm pretty sure I didn't manage to get up on that thing at any point and eventually left the rest of the gang to it and went to read my book. I don't think I managed to properly mount my board even once, and I certainly never got to say 'cowabunga'.

Later on the Saturday, we went for a drive to check out the Lisdoonvarna Matchmaking Festival, that, unbeknownst to us, was underway when we'd arrived in Lahinch. We weren't looking for love or anything, but this was probably going to be our only chance to see the festival while we had such strength in numbers. On our way there, we cranked the Christy Moore song about the town up to eleven and took great joy in imitating his famous mouth sounds. When we got bored of 'Lisdoonvarna', someone queued 'How To Save a Life' – a song that we all now saw through a different perspective. No longer a meditation on mental health and the power of talking to your mates, but instead a statement of virility and power. Like the haka, but for young Irish guys who'd rather do anything, say anything, than bring the mood down by talking about how they feel. I had my window down and my elbow resting on the beltline moulding of the car door. I shifted in my seat so I could reach the roof of the car and slap it in time with our singing. Someone else was punching the ceiling of Johnny's car. Even Cormac was all in on it and he hadn't even witnessed the jocking. We were stomping our feet so hard that I thought we might end up kicking through the floor and running to Lisdoonvarna like the Flintstones.

What sort of analysis are you supposed to apply to something like this? That a group of males spots another group of young males, some of whom behave poorly, and so the first group of males is inspired to begin emulating behaviours exhibited by the second group? Did we want to be like them? Were we making fun of them? It's entirely plausible that nobody else in the car was thinking about this. That my four friends were thinking, *What a wonderful memory I am sharing with my pals*, while I was narrowing my eyes and wondering what this all said about me as a man. But I know those guys pretty well, and they probably *were* thinking something similar.

It turned out we weren't a good fit for the Lisdoonvarna Matchmaking Festival. To this day, I'm not sure I've ever seen somewhere so densely populated by men. And I've been to battle rap events. Hell, I've been to WWE events. I went to an all-boys school. But Lisdoonvarna was the most surrounded by men I have ever felt. Apparently, this is because women are much more likely to leave their local villages for big-city jobs while men are more likely to do the kind of physical labour jobs that still exist in more rural parts of the country, contributing to a sense of loneliness among the male population of those areas. Throw in the fact that you pretty much have to drive everywhere on this island unless you live in very specific parts of it, and that many towns have little more to keep a man occupied than a pub (or a GAA club if you're fit and under the age of forty), and you start to see how so many men end up converging on an anachronism like Lisdoonvarna.

As we walked through the town, we saw that every inch of kerb space had been taken up by the parked cars of the attendees. Through the windows we could see duvets, blankets, changes of clothes, Supermac's bags. It seemed that many of the men who'd come down to the festival had eschewed traditional accommodation in favour of sleeping in their own cars, a strategy that didn't seem to lend itself very well to the prospect of romantic entanglement.

I was wearing tight black jogging pants from Zara that tapered off at the end, a choice I'd made in order to accentuate my big white runners, which I thought of as an extension of my very being. I also had on a lavender hoodie from H&M. I looked cool, goddammit. Cool! And yet, as I pushed my way through a small all-male dancefloor, I noticed that I was markedly out of place. With all the respect in the world to the male attendees of the Lisdoonvarna Matchmaking Festival, there were certain, observable patterns in their dress. Many wore blue jeans, brown shoes and shirts that looked like they could double up as tablecloths, and they were smirking at me. *This has got to be a joke*, I thought. They were dressed the way my mother used to dress me when I was five years old – and even then I was sceptical – and they thought *I* looked stupid. It is also, of course, entirely possible that my own insecurity in such a male-dominated space – all these men vying for the dozen or so women who'd shown up – was playing tricks on me. That these men were laughing because they were having a good time with each other, and not out of some desire to tear me apart with their teeth. My instincts about people being out to get me are, admittedly, almost always wrong. Once, at Electric Picnic, I'd turned to a friend and asked if he thought it strange that large Irish crowds were always so hostile. To which he replied, 'That's absolutely not the case.' Everyone I've asked since has taken his side.

Regardless, we lacked whatever social acumen was necessary to find our place in this ecosystem – besides, we weren't planning to stay long. Maybe we would have if we were cool enough, but we wouldn't have recognised this definition of cool if had it pulled our pants down in a bar while a crowd sang 'Happy Birthday' to us. Our brief stop in the town is best summed up by an incident in which Conor, who had bought himself a 99, was asked by a young woman if she could have a lick of it. Naturally, none of us knew what to do with that kind of forwardness, and so we high-tailed it out of there. The blue-jeans guys had been right to laugh.

Our next stop was the Cliffs of Moher, one of the world's least disappointing landmarks. If Fáilte Ireland needs that quote for their marketing material, they can have it for free. Three of us crawled on our bellies to the precipice while the other two filmed. Peering over the edge of a cliff into the black Atlantic Ocean, the jagged rocks and the jagged waves, either of which would put an end to you instantly. I don't remember whose idea it was to crawl, but I know I'm not smart enough to have come up with that one. I would have walked straight up to the edge and realised only too late the affect of standing upright, swaying in the autumn breeze above the black Atlantic below. Even when crawling, the abyss has a certain allure. The Book of Genesis says that we are dust and to dust we will return. But that's not true. You are water, and if there is anywhere for you to return, it's the sea. My father once told me: 'If the sea wants you, it'll get you.' Which might well be true, but it's strange advice from a man whose nautical experience mostly comprises driving onto the

Stena Line ferry at Dublin Port back when Holyhead still had a Woolworth's.

That second night, after we'd driven back to Lahinch, we ran into our young friends again, this time in a different pub. There was a faint recognition between us, the kind of respectful nod that says little more than, *Yes, I remember you from last night. Yes, I can tell that we probably have many shared cultural experiences. No, we won't kill you tonight.*

There is always a sick sense of accomplishment in the feeling of being accepted by someone who could probably eat you or snap you in half or, at the very least, make you feel very bad about yourself without trying too hard. There were no requests this night, just whatever the DJ was playing. The only song I remember was 'Zombie'. Dolores O'Riordan had died earlier that year and ever since, these late-night pub and club and house-party renditions of 'Zombie' and 'Dreams' and 'Linger' had taken on an especially sweaty aspect, like it's your duty as an Irish person to perform the hell out of them when they come on, as if we're all saying, *This is for you, Dolores.* Mercifully, the English football chant accent was left at home for 'Zombie'.

This evening on the town passed off without incident and, some time after midnight, we decamped to walk along the beachside promenade, after stopping by the apartment to pick up our remaining bottles and cans. I took one Kopparberg Mixed Fruits and stuffed the other in the marsupium of my lavender hoodie. By the time we made it back outside, the town had almost entirely emptied out. Though not quite, as we discovered when we made it to the beach.

Having strolled around the town idly, chatting and laughing and drinking our beers and playing 'Jessie's Girl' by Rick Springfield on one of our phones, doing that obnoxious thing where grown-ups hop the fence of a children's playground, jockeying on the springy horses that are bolted into the ground and, at one point, playing hopscotch, we wound down and started for our Airbnb. While mentally preparing ourselves to check out the next morning and return to our lives and jobs and a temporary dissolution of The Lads™, we noticed something.

There was this weird light off in the distance. Really bright, like light pollution bright, a beam that cut through the dead of night. As we moved closer to it, its origin became clear. The light turned towards us, like Sauron setting his gaze upon the ringbearer. It was blindingly bright by that point, and then it started flashing at us. It was an uncomfortable, jerky kind of flashing that made me think of how they do Morse code in the movies.

We could see now that the light was being operated by a

man, and towering over the man was a device for which I had no word then and have no word now. A contraption? Illuminated only by faint moonlight and the harsh but narrow white beam of whatever torchlight the man was operating, this ... thing seemed to be about 3 metres tall, planted in the sand, and bending slightly due to its own unstable dimensions. Had it been five times smaller, it might have looked like a fishing rod, but whatever it was, it was too thick, too tall, and he wasn't using it to fish. About ten yards up the beach stood another one of these objects, and both were tilted towards each other, positioned almost ritualistically, bowing together like the branches of two neighbouring trees. We continued to stare and discuss it amongst ourselves, and nobody even had a particularly good guess as to what these devices were, what their purpose could be or what this man was doing on Lahinch beach at one in the morning. Worst of all, he was with his dog (or perhaps simply *a* dog), which barked wildly as it sprinted in circles around him.

The ambience was Lovecraftian, like bearing witness to some inexplicable cultish dance. The din of an alarmed dog, the unidentified tech, the shadowy figure, the blinding light. In case you've never read H.P. Lovecraft, he has a trick he likes to pull where he says things like, 'The human mind simply cannot conceive of the horrors that came forth, and so describing them would be a waste of time', which, as a writer, I've always admired. *It was so scary that I can't describe it and you can't imagine it so let's accept it and move on and just let me do my scary story the way I want to tell it.*

Perhaps emboldened by our earlier crawl to the edge of the island, Johnny, Jamie and Cormac descended from street-level down to the beach to better stake out the scene, while Conor and I continued our walk along the prom, bidding our friends goodbye, semi-certain that in a matter of moments they would be offered up as sacrifices to the Old Gods or something.

It was a noticeably dark night. My eyes had yet to adjust to the absence of light pollution to which I'd grown so accustomed in the capital. Bands and waves of illumination emanated from the epicentre of light that was the man's torch, and we could see our friends walk towards him. The closer they got, the less in danger they seemed. I began to feel relatively reassured that we were about to get answers as to what it was we were witnessing.

Then, a few metres before they reached him, they veered off to his left and walked straight past. I didn't notice a nod, a friendly gesture or anything of the sort. Was this simply an act of cowardice or had they truly seen something that made them think better of approaching him? Conor and I exchanged a glance.

They continued along the wet sand and made for home. My frustration was gradually overtaking my fear. I wanted answers. I was, nominally, a journalist. A writer, at least notionally. Perhaps it was my responsibility to descend the steps to the beach and have a conversation with this man – who was probably normal – and ascertain the provenance and purpose of the weird rods that he had pointing towards the sky – also probably normal. Everything is probabilistically normal, after all. So, having been failed by the other three, Conor and I decided we'd hit the beach ourselves and catch up with them and, at the very least, get a closer look at this guy in the process.

It was only as we climbed down those greasy, black, stone steps that I realised the light had all but disappeared. We'd strayed too far from the man and his torch. I could barely see five feet in front of my face. I planted my feet steadily on each step, sober enough to safeguard my wellbeing in that respect, keenly aware that I could slip and break my neck. It was a treacherous little journey down, and we had entirely lost sight of our man.

I took a final step and was submerged, instantly and entirely, in freezing cold saltwater.

Where did I go wrong?

In that moment, I had no way of knowing how deep the water was, all I knew was that it was under my feet, over my head, in my nose, my eyes, my mouth, too fast for my brain to build a coherent picture of what was happening to me. What *was* happening?

The geometry of this new world was unfocused. I felt neither blind nor deaf, just seeing differently, hearing differently. There was no time for it to occur to me that I could have been turned over in the water, that if I thoughtlessly used my arms and feet to propel myself in any direction, then I could be going the wrong way. An empty night sky did nothing to delineate the surface from submersion. Was anyone going to save me? How narratively satisfying would it have been if one of the burly rugby boys, out of penance for what they'd done to that depantsed American tourist, hoisted me to safety by my waistband? Or what about the jocked man himself, proving himself a hero at the pivotal moment? What better way to cleanse your soul of a jocking than by saving a drowning man? But nobody appeared. Only instinct took me out of the water, and eventually I flopped onto the beach like a seal. I could hear Conor yelling after me but I couldn't make out what he was yelling. I wasn't taking questions, anyway.

Within less than a second, I was sprinting the length of the beach without it even crossing my mind to examine the pit that had subsumed and rebirthed me. The fall had been cold, but the shock, that sound of my body crashing into the water like a chandelier exploding into smithereens, to say nothing of the semi-urgent need to not drown, had arrested my brain's capacity to interpret signals from my body. Which is to say that, in the split-second this happened, I felt more or less fine.

It was the re-emergence that was intolerable. The night's breeze glancing and cutting across the water that clung to every inch of my body. *Fuck!* I screamed. *Fuck!* I ran. *Fuck!* I pulled my hoodie – which now weighed about a hundred times what it had minutes earlier – off my body, and my T-shirt with it. The Kopparberg Mixed Fruits that had been gestating comfortably in the pouch was gone, a meagre consolation for the Big Thing of Water that had so clearly sought a bigger and fleshier prize.

I ran in the direction of Jamie and Johnny and Cormac, suddenly conscious that the beach had reappeared, as if someone had switched on a lamp. There was no time to think about it in the moment, but that's exactly what had happened.

A text sent later to a wider group chat by Conor, who was the only first-hand witness to the fall itself, read like something from the Two-Sentence Horror subReddit: When Carl went into the water, it was pitch black, but I then saw Carl getting out of the water. That's because the torch man was illuminating us.

Whatever ritual the man had been conducting on that beach, I had undoubtedly ruined it. Whoever or whatever force this man was trying to call down into our mortal realm had surely been scared off by this shirtless, milk-pale twenty-five-year-old sprinting along the beach and screaming *Fuck!* at the top of his lungs.

When I made it to the advance party, I thrust my phone and ID into Jamie's hands and carried right on past them, making for the Airbnb, conscious that I needed to take off the rest of my clothes and get under a source of warm water quite quickly. I was experiencing a mild delirium, still unsure what on earth had just happened to me. Graciously, the other four broke into at least a jog – presumably more aware than I was that I didn't have a key to get into the apartment. It occurs to me now how fortunate we all were that the key hadn't been in my pocket or else it would probably be resting at the bottom of the Big Thing of Water and they'd have had to save me from hypothermia by taking turns cuddling me on the streets of Lahinch. One of the few things I don't remember about that trip is how my friends reacted to me running up the beach screaming and stripping off my clothes. I just remember how it felt to sit in that shower, my bones thawing out and eventually getting to a place where I was no longer saying *Fuck!* on every outbreath.

After showering, I bundled up in a duvet and headed for the couch, where the guys were playing some game on the TV in which you come up with funny answers for things, sort of like Cards Against Humanity but actually enjoyable. As I took my seat, I could see that every username and every answer centred on me falling in to what we had begun calling the Big Thing of Water, since none of us had actually seen what it was. We debated what it could have been, and I hope my friends will forgive me when I say that – in those first few hours after it happened – I believe they were sceptical as to its depths. That I was exercising a penchant for drama and contrived excitement that outstripped the reality of the Big Thing.

The next morning, we returned to the beach before our journey back to Dublin. We were in no hurry. It was a windy day. We watched seagulls attempting take-off only to find their tiny bodies caught on the breeze, suspended in midair, each one looking like a petrified bag of chips caught in an updraft. There were no mysterious rods to be found on the beach, no more panicking dog, no answers.

What we did find, however, was the set of steps Conor and I had climbed down, and what amounted to a small lagoon at the bottom of it. Visible in the surface of the steps was an iron widget that clearly, at one time or another, had been the base of steel railing along the side of the staircase. For a brief moment, I had the inherently Irish impulse to call Joe Duffy or somebody like that and tell them what a disgrace it was that there was nothing to stop people from falling off the steps. Quite quickly I realised that a railing would absolutely not have saved me. I'd stepped off the very last step and into the lagoon, and the reason I'd done so is because I was drunkenly trying to investigate the purpose of a man who I had unilaterally decided was engaged in some kind of nefarious and potentially otherworldly behaviour. This was not the fault of Clare County Council.

Based on nothing at all besides having briefly been inside of it, I had imagined the Big Thing of Water as a narrow, deep pool. A hole, essentially, perhaps dug for some infrastructural reason. Maybe something to do with whatever the torch man had been up to – a portal to an undersea world of angels and demons beyond human comprehension.

Reaching the bottom of the steps once more – now in the cold autumn daylight and wearing a pair of runners Conor had loaned me to replace my waterlogged ones – I skipped over the hole and went around to inspect it from the other side.

It was deep. I couldn't tell how deep but I couldn't see the bottom of it. The reflection of the sky was solid in the water, no thinness to suggest a bottom. Jamie took a photo of me as I knelt beside the Big Thing and, when I reviewed the picture,

I got a sense of how big this accidental lagoon was relative to my own size. You could have stood at least thirty of me side-by-side around its circumference. Face-to-face with this nameless thing, this accident, this aberration, I knew that my feelings about it were already warped. I'd spent the night thinking about it not as a body of water as we know them but as something with true agency, something that had pulled me into its depths, if not by choice then at least by some order that I don't believe I had ordained. I felt bonded to it, perhaps in the same way a fighter might develop a sense of kinship with a rival as they punch each other's faces apart.

I contemplated whether I could say that I'd come close to drowning, and I decided I couldn't. The submersion had been too brief, I had been in too much control, the water wasn't that deep. You know, the kind of things people probably think right before they start to drown.

I wondered how much drunker I'd have needed to be to drown in it, whether there'd been anything in there that I could have hit my head off, how reckless it had been of me to step blindly off a precipice onto what I assumed would be firm ground, for no better reason than the ground had always stayed beneath my feet before.

You Could Try It Once

IN HIS 1998 novel *Girlfriend in a Coma*, Douglas Coupland wrote that many young people have a tendency to live their lives as though an imaginary audience is watching.

I was seventeen when I first encountered this observation, and at the time it struck me as profound and accurate. I likely believed it was those things by virtue of its much more important property: it was applicable to me. By that age, I had already cycled through a range of personas, phases and the lifestyles thereof, permanently wrapped up in a haze of what anyone and everyone else might think of me.

I'd spent nearly three years as an emo, often misclassified while out and about as a goth or a rocker. The taxonomy of such things can be complicated. Goth carries with it the implication that I was making more of an effort with the aesthetics, while rocker suggests that I was a dedicated fan of the music. Really, I was just a sad, strawberry-blond boy with a side-fringe and a My Chemical Romance T-shirt, who spent a lot of time in CD and DVD shops trying to make eye contact with other, similarly lame teenagers who might be wearing a T-shirt of the same band, or at least a T-shirt that would have suggested a sympathy for the bands I liked.

By age fifteen, I'd done a full one-eighty and put blond highlights in my hair and started ordering clothes online from Abercrombie, figuring I'd already put in a decent shift as a non-conformist. I'd earned the right to look normal again. Around sixteen, I became more sophisticated about my aesthetic approach and started buying skinny jeans and trying to dress like The Strokes had been dressed in 2001, which actually meant trying to dress like Lou Reed and the Velvet Underground from the 1970s.

While it might have seemed, to the untrained eye, that I was undergoing many changes of personality, of preference in music and style, the more clear-eyed analyst would have seen the same thing in me at fourteen or at sixteen or at eighteen, and perhaps even now. I was neither an emo nor a jock nor a lad nor a hipster. I was a poseur. A wannabe. What exactly it was that I wanna-ed to be was always secondary to the wanting itself. An ambient yearning to be cooler than I was. Ten pounds lighter, two shades blonder, 6 inches taller, with broad shoulders like palisade walls and forearms like a tennis player, Listerine breath and perfect pitch. I wasn't cool, but I wanted people to think I was.

And then they invented social media.

Now, let's get something out of the way before we go any further. While 'social media' is the popular and universally acknowledged term for platforms such as Facebook, Twitter, Instagram and Snapchat – and even video-hosting platforms such as YouTube and TikTok – it is a term that has become dangerously outdated in the past few years. When was the last time you went on Facebook because you wanted to connect with somebody from your past? A better term for what exists now would be 'algorithmic media' – platforms where user activity is no longer dictated by the user's own social impetus, to upload and look at pictures of friends or find out what's going on in their lives or organise birthday parties, but instead to see what an algorithm has decided you should see, based on the internal machinations of a black box about which we have little or no understanding. Little more than an infinite scroll of a clown handkerchief of *lorum ipsum* gibberish that, if you were to truly immerse yourself in it, would almost certainly give you lasting brain damage. Stop calling it social media. What about this is social to you? It's algorithmic media now. With that in mind, let's proceed.

Young Irish internet users had begun their mass migration from Bebo to Facebook when I was seventeen, taking that unwitting first step towards being bound up in Meta's eventual fingertrap of communication apps. In just a few short years, the imaginary audience Coupland described was made flesh and ushered to their seats by the carnival barkers of Silicon Valley, promising connectivity, community and endless distraction – and all for free. Suddenly, the audience was not only real, but entirely essential.

To not have an audience, well, that was a strong suggestion of something amiss. A deficiency or a failure of personality. To upload albums of photos and status updates and changing your relationship status to 'Single' or 'It's Complicated' only to be ignored – not only ignored but perceptibly ignored, ignored for all to see – was a punishing sentence. Gone was the freedom of ignorance as to your exact social status. Now you could pretty much piece it together from how many people didn't wish you a happy birthday on Facebook, while others were inundated with wishes, memories, collages of photos, cryptic hints about parties you might not have been invited to. *Last night was so much fun!* Was it?

It was still a few years before there was a video camera and a high-speed internet connection in just about every pocket in the Global North, but the symptoms had begun to show. That Carveresque impulse to feel ourselves beloved on this earth and ram it down everybody else's stupid throat shone through in the form of album after album of Facebook photos celebrating every eighteenth birthday party, Leaving Cert results night, every college night out, every Mothers' Day. We soon realised there was no moment that could not be seized upon to show the world that we were as in love with our lives as it was possible to be.

Some lives emerged as more enviable than others, and, out of this stratification, the culture of influencers was born. Others found that their online currency came in the form of humour, the precursor to the 'posters' of the modern-day internet, those with a seemingly genetic predisposition towards sinking the humour they could be using to make real friends into the dopamine machine that is modern algorithmic media.

For someone who has such a hard time keeping himself offline, I have always embarrassed easily. When I was eight years old, my parents bought me a blue-and-yellow bike for my First Holy Communion – a sacrament during which I'd had to wear a full white alb – and my dad tried to teach me how to ride it on the green in front of our house. Nothing about the contraption made any sense to me. I couldn't simultaneously keep my balance and my momentum. My feet kept slipping out of the stirrups, which would then whack me on the calf and scrape up along the back of my already eczematic leg.

When I'd been even younger, I'd ridden a bike with stabilisers, but even that had proved too much of a challenge. I'd try to mount a kerb, hit the thing with a dead stop and have to jump off lest I flop flatly on my side like a Looney Tune. A Christmas or two before, I had pleaded for an Action Man scooter – and don't get me wrong, the Action Man scooter was sick as hell – but I couldn't figure out how to work the bloody thing. Same deal with skateboards: it was as if the vehicle was stuck beneath my feet, so I'd simply waddle along, dragging it behind me with my heel.

Years later, it would be discovered that I have a condition known as dyspraxia, which affects certain motor skills and coordination. The etymology of the word is interesting. It comes from Latin: *dys* meaning 'to be bad at', and *praxia* meaning 'doing'. So, to be bad at doing things. No, it's not the most hopeful name they've ever given a condition but, to be fair, they probably didn't expect any of us little bad-at-doings to look up the origin of the word.

Falling off the bike hurt badly enough, though that never bothered me. What was unbearable was the hungry gaze of the horde that hung out on the green whom I referred to ominously as 'the teenagers'.

Long before My Chemical Romance ever gave voice to the same sentiment, I was scared to death of the judgement of teenagers. To me, all of them looked like they could have been on the cover of *Top of the Pops* magazine, girls with denim jackets and Britney Spears hair, boys with wet-look spikes, scowls and eyebrow piercings. They laughed at me once or twice when I was trying to learn how to ride a bike – at least, I think they did – and that was enough for me to pack it in entirely.

My parents pleaded with me to let Dad drive us somewhere remote where I could learn without the prospect of being judged by a bunch of slightly older children, but I wasn't having it. Beyond the pangs of self-consciousness that tied up my tiny intestines, I could tell innately that this was simply not something I was capable of. The mechanics of my body seemed incompatible with those of the bike. Sure, maybe I could have learned, but never well enough to cycle alongside a car or to take myself a few towns over to visit a friend. At least not without a level of emotional and temporal investment that I deemed, even then, to be undue. If nobody else had to be so miserable about riding a bike, then why should I? At the time, it was not yet clear to me that the bike was not the cause of my misery, but that it was the apparently inherent misery that caused me to perceive the bike as an enemy.

I was also older before I realised that kowtowing to that particular neurosis probably robbed my dad of what I suspect is one of the archetypal joys of fatherhood. Even so, I'm not sure there could ever have been any other outcome. A year later, Robbie Keane scored a last-minute equaliser against Germany in the 2002 World Cup and my father picked me up and hugged me so hard I thought my ribs had broken. That was enough for me, and hopefully enough for him. Either way, the bike ended up in the shed, and I ended up on the living-room couch watching TV. I was not necessarily friendless and there were plenty of occasions when I would join in a game of football out on the green. Eventually, I even played ball with 'the teenagers'. Turns out, they weren't all that bad. TV remained the priority, though.

It was a different mode of living in the early 2000s, one that becomes less recognisable with every advancement in the technologies that have taken over virtually every facet of our lives under the guise of convenience. The dissemination of information and media had yet to be individualised to the same extent. It would be nearly two more decades before any and every digital service under the sun began claiming that it was tailor-made to your needs, because it had paid some gigantic tech firm to learn everything there is about you and people of your ilk. Back then, if you had a class of thirty children, most of them were going home to watch the same few episodes of *SpongeBob SquarePants* or *Saved by the Bell*, punctuated by the same ads for BABY Borns, Action Man scooters and package holidays to Orlando, Euro Disney or Butlin's. Sure, it wasn't quite as community-building as gathering in the village square to see the local pig thief hanged, but at least it had the effect of universalising our understanding of one another to some small degree, in one specific area.

Back in 2005, if you asked someone what they'd got up to the night before and they said they'd been watching TV, it might not have been overly revelatory as to that person's character, but it was not in any way alarming. If someone told you they spent their time watching TV, that was fine, because you watched TV too, and there was a limited amount of stuff on the TV. You were familiar with the TV, you pretty much knew every show that was on every channel, and you had some degree of certainty that there were hard limits to what the TV could and could not show.

They used to print entire magazines, whose entire purpose was to tell you what was on TV every minute of every day, mapping out every corner of the televisual landscape. You didn't need to ask anyone what they were watching, you could pretty safely assume that they were not watching some MMA-fighter-turned-misogynist-preacher or hack-pop-psychologist unload his laundry list of delusional advice for young men into the early hours of the morning. It never crossed your mind that they were watching gore or hentai. They were probably watching *Lost* or *Prison Break*. Of course, a close analysis of the timeline makes it inarguable that television created the conditions that precipitated all that we must now endure. Not only that, there was more than enough evil to be found on television. But you couldn't sneak it into your bedroom, you couldn't use it to talk to anonymous older men, it wasn't actively trying to kill you in the same way algorithmic media sometimes seems to be. In an era of such absurd violence, it's easy to miss the conventional weapons.

I fondly remember my grandfather scolding me for sitting too close to the television, warning me that my eyes would go square. That's how comparatively safe television was – grown-ups had to fabricate reasons not to watch it. Of course, that's an oversimplification, and the transition from television to algorithmic media is not exactly a mysterious one. In his 1993 essay 'E Unibus Pluram', David Foster Wallace rendered a verdict on television that cast it – though he would not have known it – as the clear precursor to the even more toxifying media that have followed in its wake. Wallace zeroed in on the idea that television was an invention for lonely people, designed to make us all lonelier. The leap from television to algorithmic media was not necessarily inevitable, but it's easy to see how our appetite for increasingly specific kinds of entertainment from all directions created the conditions that eventually led us to where we are today.

Television, especially before the advent of reality TV, was a medium through which fiction was readily identifiable as fiction, unless you were like a 1920s person watching footage of a train moving towards a camera. There were theme songs, interstitial breaks with music and b-roll, there was canned laughter, and at the end the screen went black and you could read the names of the hundreds of people who were required to make a single episode of *Sabrina the Teenage Witch*. Sure, people might have been watching television alone but, because there was little else to be doing, television could also create moments of monoculture: moon landings and All-Ireland finals, J.R. getting shot on *Dallas*, A.C. Cowlings driving his white Bronco down an Orange County freeway with O.J. Simpson in the back seat.

Maybe people *were* watching these things alone, and not with their friends, and not with their family. I am sceptical of that idea, as a generalisation. But even if they were watching alone, that's not entirely the point. We do all sorts of things alone that go on to serve a social function.

Sex, drugs, reading books – almost all of the important things we do in life we do, at least in part, so we can talk to others about them. The same was and, in many cases, remains true for TV. We watched *Sex and the City* and *The Sopranos* and *Glenroe* and Eamon Dunphy and Bill O'Herlihy (RIP) and *Big Brother* and *Game of Thrones* and *Succession* because we wanted to go into work the next day and talk about them. We use them as an excuse to text the people we fancy. If you're a millennial, you've probably sunk quite a lot of your life into doing online quizzes to tell you which character you are from the show you like. None of this is necessarily healthy or necessarily good, though it doesn't strike me as necessarily bad either.

To this very day, I watch my television in complete confidence that the little people on the other side of the glass have no idea what I'm doing. That's a job that's become tougher for modern parents, one imagines (if one is, like me, the furthest thing imaginable from a parent). A five-year-old kid carries their iPad over and asks, 'Can the people inside my iPad see me as well?' *Yeah, maybe, kid. Really depends on your settings. Put a sticker over the front camera or something.* Modern Smart TVs know our names and recognise our voices and connect to our internet. They are monitoring our habits, as are the platforms themselves. All parties involved in the watching of TV now meticulously gather data on how long we watch for, what time of day we watch, when viewers are most likely to turn something off, which episodes we skip. They give us the option of playing their shows at double-speed in case we don't really care about what's happening. Every single one of them dripping poison in our ears like the scheming eunuchs they are. *Why, sire, my wishes are of no importance ... But wouldn't you like to see Kiefer Sutherland star in a new thriller series that we'll cancel after two seasons?*

As recently as my own youth, the television set was something primitive and thoughtless and bestial, squat and dense and heavy enough to crush a toddler. You'd turn it off and it would produce a forcefield of staticky pins and needles like a warning to stand clear. The televisions of the 1990s have about as much place in the modern world as a grandfather clock or the *Golden Pages*.

Still, the television as a mode of media consumption offered us something significantly more egalitarian than we have become accustomed to in the age of hyper-individualisation. First and foremost, the TV showed the same ads to young and old, rich and poor alike. In 2003, when you watched Richard Hillman try to kill Gail Platt and her kids by ploughing his Ford Galaxy into the canal, you were having more or less the same experience as everyone else who had tuned in.

There were rudimentary attempts to target ads in those days, sort of like a clunky blunderbuss version of what we have today. Things like gambling ads on the sports channels, or how when you'd stay home sick from school you'd get to see all the ads for things that old people seemingly cared about, like commemorative coins or life-insurance policies that were so good that the kindly British people talking about them actually seemed like they were welcoming the sweet embrace of death for the pittance it would earn their loved ones. Otherwise, we were all more or less getting the same ads.

This was a time when ads had developed a cultural cachet of their own, regularly penetrating the mainstream and shaping the way we talk for years afterwards. To this day, it's still easy to get a cheap laugh by trotting out well-remembered advertising catchphrases like 'I don't know what a tracker mortgage is' or '*Tabhair dom an cáca milis*'. If you were to conduct a straw poll of people exactly my age and ask them what associations they have with the songs 'Body II Body' by Samantha Mumba or 'Just One Look' by Linda Ronstadt, I am confident that, to a person, they would give the same answer (the answer being 'I associate those songs with being shown staged footage of young people getting obliterated by cars in the name of road safety'). There was only so much TV to go around.

As a concession to second-screen syndrome – the phenomenon whereby new TV shows and movies are written in such a way that characters explain what they do as they're doing it because they know everyone sitting at home isn't actually looking at the TV, but passively absorbing it in bits and pieces in between playing addiction games on their phone, opening and closing and reopening apps like a hungry man with an empty fridge – you have my permission to temporarily divert your attention away from this book, visit Twitter, type any topical keyword into the search bar, and spend five minutes reading as many tweets as you can. Go ahead.

Are you back? See what I mean? *Lorum ipsum dolor sit amet.* Pain sits here, indeed.

On top of this deluge of content, we are also now lucky enough to be 'served' personalised ads, obsequious and derisory things that try to hide themselves amongst our regular diet of information consumption. Subliminal messaging done badly. Done backwards, even. Rather than nudging us into buying anything, now the ad companies listen to what we want and then show us an ad for it the next time we check Instagram, with the gall to act like it was their idea. *You're only showing me hammocks because I already told you I want one.* It's like if Don Draper lived under your bed.

Given this discrepancy in the information environment – that all of us are seeing different content, content intentionally chosen to appeal to a model of our exact, specific brain – one might expect millennials and the generation that has followed, known as Gen Z or zoomers, to be unbridgeably different. It's certainly what many newspaper columnists and casual anecdotes would have you believe. Zoomers don't like to work, we're told. Zoomers don't like to drink. Zoomers don't like to fuck. Some accounts would give you the unambiguous impression that Gen Z is rewriting human nature itself.

I've always been sceptical as to whether analysing sociological phenomena through a generational lens is the best way to go about things. It may be more useful for future generations, since informational borders are eroding thanks to our shared inhabitation of the same handful of digital platforms, and this might make the content you consume more integral to your identity than, say, the country where you were born.

Even if we were to accept that our 'generation' is determinative of the kind of cultural content we consume and therefore formative in the foundation of our personality, it still seems awfully crude that we put brackets around every fifteen-year period, as if someone born in 1997 has some inherent and immediately identifiable commonality with someone else born, perhaps on the other side of the world, perhaps in entirely incomparable socio-economic circumstances, in an entirely different body, to an entirely different family, in 2012. At least astrology has the decency to pretend there's some sort of science to it. When it comes to sorting people by generation, how does it make any sense to group people born in 1998 with those born fourteen years after them before you group them with the people who were born five years before them? Granted, nobody wants to return to the ''90s kid' identity gimmick that was so common in the early 2010s, but it's worth making the point that grouping people by the decade they were born in — from zero to zero — makes just as much sense as whatever we're doing now.

If we've really decided that this age-based way of thinking about people is sensible, when exactly did we decide how long a 'generation' was supposed to last? It's a fuzzy logic problem. You have a pile composed of 100,000 grains of sand. If you remove one grain of sand, you have a pile composed of 99,999 grains of sand. If you keep removing grains of sand one by one, eventually you'll only have three grains of sand ... two grains of sand. Is it still a pile of sand then? Most would argue not but, if not, then when did it cease to be a pile and enter some new, distinct category in your mind? How few grains of sand must there be for this collection of sand to lose the property of pile-ness? When does one generation end and a new one begin? Why every fifteen years and not every ten years? Every five years? Why don't we start doing it by the Chinese zodiac, so I can go pal around with all my rooster buddies who – by the logic of generational analysis – should share the most in common with me?

We might not like to believe it, but go to a far-right rally anywhere in the world and you'll find people of all generations there. Men of all generations hurt and kill women. People of all generations play their part in upholding structures of oppression, cruelty, exploitation and genocide the world over. In terms of harmful indolence, there are probably few examples more egregious than the song Whitney Houston covered, about believing the children are the future. I mean sure, that is true in the tautological sense, but we've had about four new generations since that song was first released in 1977. We talk about new generations as though we're addicts. Please, let us name and ascribe a bunch of attributes to just one more generation. Let us set one more generation of teens against one more generation of thirtysomethings. That'll solve it all.

Despite my keen awareness that millennials are a painfully cringe and earnest generation, I do feel there were clear advantages to being born exactly when I was. For example, when I hear 'Steal My Sunshine' by Len or 'Breakfast at Tiffany's' by Deep Blue Something or 'Two Princes' by the Spin Doctors, or pretty much anything by Third Eye Blind, Barenaked Ladies or Counting Crows, I am filled with certainty that I was chosen by God. All of these songs were written and recorded by Gen X slackers, sure, and I'm also sure that the xillennials (someone on the border of Generation X and millennial – a category that immediately gives the lie to the whole fucking idea, by the way) believe that those songs were written for them. But they would be wrong about that.

The purest way to appreciate a song like 'Breakfast at Tiffany's' is to be five years old in the back seat of your family's 1989 Renault as its opening notes become embedded in your source code for the rest of your life. Genuinely, go find someone who's thirty-two years old and unexpectedly start playing the first few seconds of 'Come With Me' or 'Better Off Alone' and see how excited they get. There's a phrase people like to use online these days: 'This rewired my brain.' People say it when they like something because it's not enough just to say that you like something anymore. The thing you like must be iconic. It must be everything, or there's really no reason to even get out of bed for it.

The kind of pop music they made in the 1990s was decidedly uniconic. You listen to the improvised spoken intros to the verses of 'Steal My Sunshine' ('Sharon, I love y—') and you cannot conclude that these people even had aspirations of being 'everything'.

As with much else, pop music in the modern era has been monopolised by behemoth corporations who have concentrated all of the attention towards a select few artists at the very top, and everyone else is pretty much a nobody. Small venues are dying out across the world and the costs of making music, performing music, doing music in any meaningful way continue to rise disproportionately against wages. Nobody is making tracks like 'Steal My Sunshine' anymore. Sure, it's not exactly the number one most serious consequence of this new mode of living, but it's an illustration of what is being lost. In order for a band like Len to get 'Steal My Sunshine' off the ground now, they'd at the very least need to come up with an accompanying dance to lend to the track's viral credentials and turn it into an audiovisual social package that outstrips the song itself. Everyone still loves music, don't get me wrong, but they love it an awful lot more when there's a fully integrated and interactive marketing campaign to go with it.

Fall into the wrong part of your Instagram or TikTok 'For You' page and you'll see the kind of people who are trying to penetrate pop stardom through the digital platforms and the kinds of things they're doing to achieve their dreams. The smarter cookies among them will zero in on one specific relatable theme. They'll write a song about kissing a girl in the front row at their concert, then they'll film a concert where they play that song, and kiss a girl in the front row. Then they'll do that 500 more times in the hopes that one of their videos will impress people enough to achieve virality. They'll film themselves busking – often in a way that is decidedly intrusive, obnoxious and uncanny – thereby guaranteeing the kind of hate-clicks that serve as propulsion for the dissemination of modern content.

I don't know what kind of effect this is having on young people who have little to no frame of reference for what culture used to be like before it turned into a permanently rebounding and ricocheting scrap for attention above all else. Maybe that's unsatisfying to you. Maybe you expected me to write intelligently about the habits of people still in their first flush of youth. Personally, I've always found commentators and columnists who overly concern themselves with the behaviour of children to be deeply unchic. I don't care what the kids are doing unless they're planning a 1966-esque cultural revolution where they pull millennials out of their homes and beat them to death. Until they're armed and at my door, you can pretty much leave me out of it.

As a millennial myself, I am loathe to speculate on the state of the Gen Zs for a few reasons. Chief among them is this: it's only been a few short years since the crazy-making and fear-mongering headlines were not about zoomers but millennials. Here is a quaint and cursory overview:

Millionaire to Millennials: Stop Buying Avocado Toast If You Want To Own a Home (*Time* magazine, 15 May 2017)

Why Aren't Millennials Buying Diamonds? (*The Economist*, 1 July 2016)

Millennial Dads Have Pathetic DIY Skills Compared To Baby Boomers (*New York Post*, 6 June 2019)

Millennials and Gen Z Are Fighting Again. This Time About Gym Clothes. (*The New York Times*, 17 March 2025)

I included that final example to illustrate a few things. First, that even the most prestigious publication on the planet is unable to rise above playing this game of generational divide and conquer. Second, that this kind of journalism is still being produced now. Third, if *The New York Times* is pumping out bullshit like this, it's because people read it.

Not Gen Z-ers, of course. If you're to believe everything you read about the zoomers, they have no interest in reading, can't understand any text written in anything but the first person, and, in many cases, are functionally illiterate. Of course, if you believed everything you read about millennials, you'd have been wrong as well.

It is no longer fun to point out the ironies that undergird all of these headlines. Enough people have done the maths on avocado toast and iced-caramel lattes to prove a million times over that you can't substitute either for a house. It should be clear by now that millennial spending habits, preferences with respect to prioritising 'work–life balance' over traditional metrics of success, and whatever else, were simply a response to forces and trends that go well beyond being possessed by some animus that poisoned the minds of all children born between 1981 and 1996 against home ownership, weddings big enough that relatives you've never met can come and diamonds.

Millennials were the first generation to grow up with search engine access to information, the only cohort whose early development was bisected by the introduction of Google's search bar, an event no less cataclysmic than if the Library of Alexandria had managed to piece itself back together from the ash. Younger people will only know Google as it exists now, infested with ads designed to distract you from your original purpose and misdirect you in such a way that you don't even realise your time is being harvested, shorn from the stalk right under your nose as you sit there wondering why googling the word 'skyscanner' doesn't produce the 'SkyScanner' website as the top result anymore. The popular term for this process is 'enshittification'– a word that we'll probably all know by the end of the decade as the tech monopolies continue to degrade the quality of their products with less and less shame. Millennials will always be able to look back on a version of Google that was able to convert metres into inches without any further instruction, something that Google has forgotten how to do now, instead taunting us with insane calculations, behaving a little bit like a whale at SeaWorld right before it snaps and turns on an audience member. You would wonder if those responsible fear for their souls, but it is likely that they believe it will soon be possible for AI to generate a needle with an eye wide enough to allow the passage of 10,000 camels abreast.

Having the history of information to hand often reminds me of a story my uncle once told me. He'd been travelling Morocco in the late 1980s or early 1990s and while boarding a train, he'd overheard someone saying that Nelson Mandela had died. Naturally, he was shocked, but the news drifted from his mind over the course of the journey, and when he disembarked in Casablanca or wherever, he simply went about his life. He didn't learn that Nelson Mandela had been alive all along until much later.

There is a well-known sociological phenomenon known as the Mandela effect, which refers to a situation in which a large and disparate group of people all remember a historical event or artefact the wrong way. Like, for example, if I were to tell you to picture the Monopoly man and you picture him wearing a monocle? You, my friend, are a victim of the Mandela effect. The Mandela effect is so named because many people seem to remember Nelson Mandela dying long before he actually did. In this day and age, it seems a strange thing, but it shouldn't be. Of course these people had no idea whether or not Nelson Mandela was dead. They had no way to immediately check. Do you, personally, keep an internal

Rolodex of all the world's significant figures and whether they are dead or alive? Knowing precisely who is dead or alive is an entirely new feature of modern life and while it feels innate to us, it absolutely isn't. It is something we would lose access to tomorrow if we woke up and discovered that screens don't work anymore. It would be like an episode of *The Twilight Zone*, all of us marching zombified through the streets grabbing each other by the lapels and screaming things like, 'Is Michael Douglas dead? Tell me if he's dead, you son of a bitch.' A utopia.

Us millennials, the youngest generation to have lived with and without this kind of power, born on the double-edged sword as it were, probably could have made ourselves useful. We could have performed our role as canaries in the coalmine more diligently, flopped down dead more dramatically, so that the miners couldn't ignore us. Perhaps our cries for help would have been heard more clearly had they not been couched between our insistence on arranging each other into the Hogwarts houses, partaking in flashmobs and generally cementing the perception of ourselves as the most irritating generation to ever walk the planet – including the generations that seemed to be pretty much entirely comprised of war criminals.

By taking such a zoomed-out approach and thinking of ourselves only as 'millennials' and by separating ourselves from the so-called generation that has followed, people who in many cases are less than half a decade our junior, we make it pretty much impossible to get to the truth of anything. Generational analysis is very useful for people who love to outrage others. It's a time-honoured thing, to tell the younger generation that they're a bunch of pussies. Millennials have already started doing it to the zoomers. Anecdotally, we believe that they are reluctant to work and impossible to manage. That they don't know how to save files to a desktop computer. That they are hopelessly incapable of socialising, that their men are more likely to be at home planning a mass-shooting event than chatting to a woman in a club. The older people get, the less time they have for the kind of questions that could make them doubt their course. That's reasonable. As with any journey, the closer you get to the midpoint, the less sense it makes to turn around.

However, this headlong rush for a sense of stasis always seems to be thrown out of whack by the behaviour of a younger generation whose preferences diverge from the expectations of the previous generation. We think their slang is silly, we think their attitudes are entitled, we cannot for the life of us understand how bootcut jeans came back into fashion and skinny jeans became off-putting and embarrassing. We believe that we have it figured out, and until the hands of time bitchslap us and remind us that we didn't have it figured out any better than the generations that came before us. And have you seen what a shitshow those guys were?

One bold call that I am prepared to make about Gen Z, and indeed Generation Alpha already following closely behind, is that they are lonely kids. I'm confident in making this statement because I know that millennials were lonely kids, and there's absolutely nothing to suggest that this state of affairs has improved. None of us are necessarily lonely because of when we were born or because it's hard to buy a house or financially imprudent to have children or because marriage no longer seems worthwhile. We're lonely because the world is a lonely place by its nature, and there isn't a generation that hasn't been preoccupied with finding the means to plug the holes that seem to emerge in the human heart as a matter of course.

Since ancient times, those outlets have involved performance, some sense of occasion. Bread, circuses, etc. As culture continues to break apart into tinier pieces, with every TikTok creator, every YouTuber, every Twitch streamer holding on to their own tiny smithereen of the zeitgeist, that sense of occasion has been lost. The pageantry, the catharsis. Where once media tried to show us unlikely scenarios of violence, grief, terror, sex, love and excitement, what we produce now is resolutely confined to relatability. There are successful comedians, boasting enough followers to make Jim Jones and David Koresh look like amateurs, who have never told a single joke. They just open up their phone camera and say things like 'Don't you hate when you forget your wifi password?' Sometimes they'll get their wife to be in the video, and she'll frustratedly read the wifi password. This will go back and forth for a little while until the video just sort of ... ends. That's the kind of material that these days could win you hundreds of thousands of likes on Instagram, a full audience of the face-with-tears-of-joy emoji.

The real difference between TV and the digital platforms is that there's an awful lot more money to be made by sucking you into your phone for seven hours a night than there ever was in producing TV shows. Meta, TikTok and YouTube don't need to make anything besides the algorithms they cook up in their labs like Adrian Veidt lovingly designing that enormous laser-beam squid that destroys New York at the end of *Watchmen*. The success of just about anything at all is dependent upon favourable treatment by those algorithms.

Once upon a time, there were indie record labels, indie movie studios, all free from the diktats of the major label. Now, good luck finding an independent company that isn't almost entirely reliant on Instagram or TikTok for publicity. The very concept of independence has been eroded, and everything has become contingent. What this means is a media landscape saturated with total shit, without any guardrails for quality control, and addictive content that almost uniformly makes people less thoughtful, less creative, less interested and, apparently, quite content.

The real difference between Gen Z and millennials? They've been failed even worse than we were, and we were failed pretty fuckin' badly.

This is not a charts-and-graphs kind of book, but more than enough evidence has been produced to prove that diminishing returns have long since set in when it comes to quality of life. When I was a child, it seemed utterly unthinkable that such societal vital signs like life expectancy would either stall or reverse in the way we are seeing in the Western world. It was simply never suggested that it would soon cost us ten times the median national salary to buy a small house in an unsalubrious neighbourhood. We were naïve enough to think it farfetched that yet another genocide could be perpetrated before our eyes and that entire bloc of democratically elected governments would sit on their hands in between selling weapons and doing trade with those responsible. Foolish enough to think that there were enough of us committed to upholding the public good against the avaricious will of capital that simple human faculties – such as discerning truth from obvious lie – could be protected. We know now that we live in a world that is unjust, and unjustifiable. That anyone who thrives within this paradigm should at least have the decency to feel deeply ashamed of themselves.

Stabilisers or no, we have hit the kerb and toppled over, and too many of us now seek to remedy the problem by taking to the couch, seeking our comforts: the voices and faces and bodies of people half a world away, churning whatever it is we need to keep us numb.

Timelines, For You pages, podcasts – these things demand solitude. People are no more likely to listen to a podcast with someone else than they are to sit side-by-side on a bench each reading from the same book. Yet the purpose of so many modern podcasts seems to be the very subversion of loneliness. When podcasts first came to prominence with the explosion of *Serial*, a purposeful investigation into a murder and possible case of miscarried justice, the medium was in its infancy. While true crime has certainly remained core to the appeal of podcasts – though the genre almost immediately became diluted, ethically shady and morally repugnant – the real money is in podcasts about nothing at all. Two or three guys or girls sitting around a table with their mics plugged in and their 7D camera switched on, because it's not enough to *hear* Joe Rogan try to think for himself in real-time while a Lyle Lanley type swindles him into drinking horse dewormer, we have to *see* Joe Rogan try to think for himself. We want to see the beads of sweat bursting through the porous pinholes on his big bald head as he furrows his brow at Jordan Peterson and tries to work out if what the guy is saying is some kind of parable or actually real.

Nobody is learning anything from Joe Rogan. I'll go as far as to say that nobody is ever learning anything from that kind of podcast, because learning isn't the point, and entertainment isn't really the point either. The point is familiarity, the tone and the timbre of voice you've grown to associate with feelings of comfort, the lowlight of your bedroom in the evening or the peace of your kitchen as you chop vegetables for dinner. A voice that tells you, my beautiful, monetisable audience, that you are smart, you are wise, you are included. And you are definitely not imaginary.

At Least It Looks Good From Space

I'VE BEEN SLEEPING a lot lately. For the past twenty years, if I'm being honest. Sometimes, I wonder if I'm addicted to sleep. I know that 'addicted' probably isn't the right word. You probably can't be addicted to sleep like you can be addicted to alcohol or cocaine or something real, something that tears lives apart. I don't mean to trivialise real addictions. I know that whatever I've got going on can't be a real addiction. I just don't know another word for when your body wants something it shouldn't have all of the time, all of the time.

If you ask Google whether you can be addicted to sleep, it will tell you that you can't, but that it might be a sign of an underlying condition, which is what Google always says, and I suppose one day it will eventually be correct, and that will be that. I don't think my relationship with sleep is the result of some malignant physical condition, though. I've got my bloods done a couple of times in recent years. I assumed, hoped actually, that I would be deficient in something. Anaemic, possibly. Maybe I'd have scurvy. I don't know what you'd call my diet, but I guarantee you there are some essential food groups missing in there.

When the results came in, it was bad news: I was totally fine, getting absolutely enough of everything. So, I guess this sleep thing is more of a personality problem. Besides, I can't pretend that the issue is simply that I sleep a lot. It's that I actively want to sleep a lot. I yearn for it. In the same way that some people crave a pint after work, I daydream about the time I will get to dream for real. Recently, an ex-partner of mine asked me what theme song I'd choose for myself and I didn't even need to think about it. 'Daysleeper' by R.E.M., without question.

I regard my seemingly limitless capacity for sleep as a kind of talent. You might disagree, but you'd change your mind if you saw me fold myself in half from the middle like a napkin and sleep doubled-over through a forty-five-minute flight between Dublin and London.

On any given morning after waking up, I could just as easily close my eyes and keep sleeping indefinitely. Sleep itself is like a blanket I can pull over my shoulder, that, even as gravity tugs it to the floor, I can clasp and hold fast to me, and fall back asleep. It is very rare that I experience FOMO, because I am so automatically comforted that even if I'm not at Electric Picnic watching Nile Rodgers play 'Le Freak' to an Irish audience for the thousandth time since he realised that we're the easiest marks on the planet, I can take great consolation in being asleep. Not that it would bother me to sleep on a flimsy tent floor on top of the wet autumn grass while the rain drips in through the canvas. It wouldn't bother me to sleep anywhere at all. Why should I be bothered? I'd be asleep. I think Epicurus said something like that once, though he might have been talking about death.

Similarly, my body seems to regard a lack of sleep as a sort of primordial threat. On rare occasions when I stay awake late enough that the sun comes up, the dawn chorus will invariably trigger a fight-or-flight response in my body. I'm wincing just thinking about it. Throughout my adult life – college, work, creative projects – I have budgeted for at least a hundred all-nighters, and I have never successfully completed a single one. If you scroll through my phone, you'll find an alarm set at pretty much every five-minute interval throughout the day because there has been virtually no time of day at which I have not, at some point, been worried that I was about to fall asleep. It is this system of alarms that keeps me gainfully employed and preserves my status as a semi-functioning member of society.

Because of the lust for sleep that I build up over the course of a day from the moment I wake, I end up actively choosing sleep over doing important things, like being on time for pretty much anything that it won't get me fired to be late for, sustaining promising romantic relationships or being a real person who does things for other people in his spare time instead of feeding all of that free time into the yawning maw of some blind, grasping, seductively warm sleep god.

This is not a new phenomenon for me. When I was in secondary school, I would set an alarm for at least thirty minutes before I had to wake up for real so I could briefly regain just enough consciousness to register the physical sensations that come with sleep, my central nervous system still effectively smothered, trying to hold off as long as possible before my brain started clanging like an old-timey town crier going through the streets bellowing 'Hear ye! Hear ye! Get out of bed, you lazy fuck.' Holding myself in that state of potentiality, between the pliable and pleasing architecture of dreams and the cold and unforgiving momentum of morning, was a challenge, and a skill that I actively sought to sharpen. Eventually, my father resorted to throwing wet towels at me to get me out of bed. Good holy God, I hope those weren't used towels.

As life began to allow for further lie-ins – college days when class wouldn't start until midday, jobs where shifts didn't start until the afternoon – I embraced the extra sleep that found its way into my schedule. Besides, now that I was a working man I needed the sleep an awful lot more.

I spent most of my time in college working in an underground car park in a high-end south Dublin shopping centre, the kind of vaguely unsafe and pointless busywork that would make any soot-faced nineteenth-century urchin look on in envy. My uniform consisted of a short-sleeved burgundy bowling-style shirt and a clip-on tie in the very same colour, worn tucked tightly into the very same grey slacks that had been part of my secondary school uniform for the Junior Cert cycle. I wore a pair of steel-toed boots that I got at Guineys and a hi-viz jacket to make sure the cars didn't hit me.

The job demanded little more than being on my feet in an enclosed space with thousands of cars driving in and out. One time, a co-worker wiped his finger on a seemingly clean wall to illustrate the black, ashy exhaust that had collected on his fingertip. 'That's what the inside of our lungs looks like,' he said. I have no idea if he was correct, but I do remember the weekend they had some people in to do air purity tests, and I remember even more keenly that we were never shown the results. We got quarterly bonuses, for some reason (car parks are apparently austerity-proof) and I got a manual-handling certification out of it, so overall it was probably a draw. It's over a decade later, and my lungs still seem to be holding up.

My few duties in the car park included hanging around near the pay stations in the event that somebody lost their parking ticket, in which case I would push the 'Press for Assistance' button on the pay station and explain the situation to the control room. Those in the control room would print a new ticket, and I would be thanked as a hero for my efficiency and my grace in handling the situation. Occasionally, we'd get troublemakers. The kind of folk who think that just because they can pay €2 an hour for parking and think nothing of it that means they can spit on us highly visible mole-people who toil from Level -3 to the dizzy heights of the second-floor mezzanine.

One day, my colleague and I spotted an elderly man sitting in the passenger seat of a car that was blocking a loading bay. We went over and politely let him know that he should ideally move the car as soon as possible, and he told us kindly that he was just waiting for his wife to come back and he'd move it as soon as she returned. We were happy enough with that, but when we circled back fifteen minutes later, he was still sitting there. We asked him if there was any sign of his wife because, by that time, the control room was breathing down our necks trying to get the guy to move. He told us that his wife was just getting an ice cream and she'd be in the car when she was done. This seemed entirely reasonable – who doesn't like ice cream? – so we went on our way again. Some ten minutes later, we could see that the car was still in the same place, and that the wife was now sitting in the passenger seat, chatting jovially with her husband. For a third time, we journeyed over to remind the couple that they had to move, at which point the old man looked up at us from behind a cone topped with a strawberry pink scoop and indignantly said, 'Well, you can hardly expect me to drive when I'm eating my ice cream.' You win this round, old man.

Sometimes, people would crash their cars, other times cars would catch fire of their own accord. One time, a woman drove over a whole flexi-bollard that got stuck in the undercarriage of her car and when I explained to her what had happened she looked me dead in the eye and said, 'Well, it wasn't there when I made the turn.'

For the most part, people just needed help figuring out

what level they had parked on, which you could usually ascertain by asking them either what road they'd taken to get to the shopping centre, or which store they walked into first. Only once did a woman threaten to call Joe Duffy on me, and I suffered no professional consequences for the time I locked dozens of people in an overflow car park for an amount of time that was never actually made clear to me.

It was a job that taught me that I lack a natural aptitude for endurance, and that I find the pressure of my own body weighing on my joints over the course of a day to be basically intolerable. I remember dragging my torn-up steel-toed boots along those floors, so slick they were practically laminated. I think about the hours I spent alone with my own thoughts, roaming row after row of empty cars, constantly shifting my weight from hip to hip, hiding in the stairwell to take my shoes off and watch the steam rise off the floor as I flatted my soles against the cool grey concrete. Eventually, I got a smartphone, which eased the pain. This was a primitive time for the technology and rather than use it to stream, which I highly doubt that old HTC was capable of, I simply refreshed the BBC livescore page over and over in the hope that Liverpool might have scored.

One weekend, we had a fire-safety drill during which it was explained to us what our role would be in evacuating the centre should it ever catch fire, and I wondered very sincerely how much these people thought I cared about this car park, and this shopping centre. *Look, man, I'll save whoever I can on the way out but if this place goes up in flames, I will be walking directly to safety through the enormous multi-lane exit 10 metres away.*

I acquired only two skills from my time in the car park. The first is that manually counting down the seconds and minutes of my day has given me a very keen instinct for what time it is. If you ask me at any time of day what the time is, I'll be able to give you a relatively accurate answer. And I know what you're thinking! 'That's not an impressive skill!' Yes, you're correct.

The second skill I honed was my eye for trolleys left in car parks that still have a euro in them. This skill is very useful, and seems to extend to all car parks, not just the one I worked in for three years. Sadly, I've forgotten everything I ever learned about manual handling.

Either way, the work wore me out, and I responded to that not by improving my diet or my core strength or taking any proactive measure to ameliorate the situation but instead by sleeping more. Sleeping as late as I could, in fact, until the moment that I could sleep no longer owing to the unjust demands of the working world. The car-park managers were sticklers for timekeeping. In the years since, I've found most employers are kind of that way about being on time. How embarrassing. *Oh no, what happens if I'm late? Will the cars stage a mutiny against us? Grow up. I'll be there before lunch.* It seems that while other people were in the infancy of understanding what work–life balance meant to them, counterweighing work with pursuits like exercise or drinking or some other real-life thing, I was applying my focus to sleep. Some people take up running but, when you think about it, sleeping is the real running and, if you're asleep, then nobody can ever catch you.

I left my job in the car park in the summer of 2014, but the sleeping matter intensified, as many matters did, during the Covid-19 pandemic. The first Covid case in Ireland was confirmed the day after I turned twenty-seven. I had been so looking forward to joining the twenty-seven club – the club of people who'd had a hard time up until the age of twenty-seven but then suddenly managed to turn it around, survive the year and go on to live happy and fulfilling lives. That plan went out the window.

It's easily forgotten how confused we were right before it got serious. The incongruity of it all. Thousands of Irish punters flying over and back to Cheltenham in the same week that the Italians sent their army into Bergamo because the health workers there could no longer process the tonnage of corpses. In the early days, there was even vacillation from global public-health officials on whether or not wearing an N95 mask would make any difference. Sat around a board game in our family's back room, we discussed a *Business Post* headline that reported a projection that 1.9 million Irish people would end up falling ill with the novel coronavirus. 'Well, that means all of us will get it,' I remember saying huffily, as though there had hitherto been some reason to believe my loved ones and I would be exempted from this highly contagious airborne virus.

Still, despite my moody teenager routine – a pouty little posture I reflexively settle into whenever I spend more than a week at home – I was still too ignorant to truly despair. Though I am not an optimist by nature, a childhood spent getting worked up every time a chicken got the flu and being forced to write letters to Tony Blair pleading with him to shut down Sellafield before the nuclear waste runoff turned me into a mutant (thanks for nothing, Adi Roche) meant that I was pretty much all panicked out by the time Covid came around.

In the first week of March 2020, I told my brother that a trip we had planned for later in the month wouldn't be cancelled because 'if it were cancelled that would mean that Covid is the biggest thing to have ever happened, and obviously it's not going to be the biggest thing that ever happened'. At the time, he nodded along, gratefully accepting the sage-like advice of his wise older brother. I don't think he's made the same mistake since. I'm not sure if Covid was the biggest thing that's ever happened, but it's definitely top five in my lifetime and, let me tell you, that's a competitive field.

As it became clear that this was no ordinary SARS or H1N1, I wondered if life would start to feel a little more like the end of the world than usual. One evening, I went for a run around my 2-kilometre radius – probably one of the few Covid measures that we can all now agree didn't make very much sense – past a garda checkpoint that had been set up on a nearby quiet suburban road. Passing the church on my way home, I wondered why nobody was in there praying. Bargaining. *Shouldn't we be beating the door down? Isn't now the time? Where have all the guys wearing 'The End Is Nigh' sandwich boards gone? They were right all along; this is their moment for a victory lap. Maybe they've already been raptured.*

It was not like any end of the world I'd imagined before. The sky didn't change colour, motorways didn't split open like KitKat bars, rivers didn't burst their banks and crash through windows, flowers weren't blooming in reverse. Early in the pandemic, when we knew it was a pandemic but there were still more people with Covid on cruise liners bobbing in perpetuity off the world's coastlines than there were in many countries, I would sit at my laptop and watch the Johns Hopkins University Covid map, a black atlas where incidents of Covid were mapped out in a deep red, like blood from a stab wound spreading across the fibres of a new shirt. I would take the number of cases in Iran or Peru and divide them by the overall population of the territory, and I would briefly feel comforted. The multiplier effect had yet to kick in, but it would. The end of the world doesn't come for us all at once, just a few of us at a time.

It wasn't much of a challenge for me to confine my social life to the house. A lot of people seemed to feel that way, and they seemed to think it was terribly amusing. There was a lot of aggressively millennial humour floating around online at the time to that effect. *Social distancing? Been there, done that.* Like 'gin o'clock' content for the belligerently lonesome.

To my shame, it was also true of me. The social ramifications of Covid didn't really stress me out, and I always found it pretty easy to get on board with whatever safety directives were issued. Besides, the advent of Zoom and Discord and various other chat platforms created a new opportunity for many Irish people. Since finishing college, at least a dozen of my good friends had left the country, joining the emigrant enclaves in London, Vancouver, New York, Berlin, Edinburgh and elsewhere. This has been a relatively standard state of affairs for Irish people since the Brits starved so many of us to death in the middle of the nineteenth century, an event that has since been popularly recharacterised as a 'famine'.

Until Covid descended upon us, my friends and I had never really thought to do a video call. I suppose you learn who your real friends are when the very concept of geographical distance is rendered irrelevant for six months. As it turns out, my real friends were exactly who I thought they were, and The Lads™ and I settled firmly into a Saturday-night routine of figuring out which board games we could play online and getting thoroughly hammered while we took turns fucking each other over on *Settlers of Catan*. I was new to the game and I have no mind for strategy whatsoever but God help me I love to barter. From what I could tell, the point of *Catan* was to accumulate sheep, eventually swap them for bricks, and graciously congratulate my friends on whooping my ass again. *Catan* became a big part of my life and, before long, I was playing solo games against three CPU avatars with names like Hildegaard. I even spent €3 on a little avatar that looked like a llama. Wasn't much else to be spending it on, let me tell you.

The objective of *Catan* is to earn points by building settlements and cities and roads, and playing it took me back to the good old days of my childhood spent as a rollercoaster tycoon. Before and after the *Catan*, though, my friends and I would talk. Each call would kick off with us holding up and showing off our bottles or cans, as though my six pack of Tennent's was some kind of precious prison contraband rather than simply a strange early pandemic-induced phase I was going through. Though each of us was living under lockdown measures that gave us very little to do, I found that we became more fulsome at updating each other as to the minutiae of our lives, comparing restrictions in our various cities. We all became very invested in each others' Lego projects. Cormac even built a functioning lamp from scratch.

It was in that deep, shared boredom that many people around the world were surely reminded of just how much they like their friends. How wonderful it is to hear about someone's trip to their hole-in-the-wall coffee kiosk, to listen as they leave their keyboard to make themselves lunch because they were calling in from a timezone seven hours behind, to have them review the bottled cocktail they'd taken away from some small hipster business on the verge of going under. As someone who has always felt that physical contact is overrated, I found that hanging out with my friends over Discord was more intimate and more intentional than the corporeal alternative, nice as it would have been to see them. And, besides, I was getting kind of good at *Catan*.

Some nights we would drink and talk for so long that some of us would fall asleep on camera. It was the first time in a long time that I felt like the internet had been useful for something. Our video calls formed part of the ritualism that took hold of everyone in those early months.

Perhaps the most universal expression of this ritualism was the clamour for 'the numbers' each day. That's what you'd ask people: 'Jesus, did you see the numbers?' Every day, Chief Medical Officer Dr Tony Holohan and a revolving cast of public-health officials would tell us how many people had died with the illness, how many people were in hospital with the illness, how many people were in ICU with the illness. Occasionally, they would release a county-by-county breakdown of the figures. The country was riveted by this, extrapolating all sorts of things from the data — primarily how fucked we were. Listening out for the numbers felt like stepping into footage of wartime families sitting around one of those old-timey radios that looks like a microwave without a door. As the year wore on, the cases climbed to truly frightening heights. There is a palpable push now to revise the reality of Covid, and downplay the damage it did across the country. On 20 April 2020, no fewer than seventy-seven people were confirmed to have died with the virus in Ireland in one day.

The weekly sessions with my friends were a necessary distraction from the pervading sense of hopelessness that defined those first few months when we still had no idea how many people the virus would kill, how long we would be locked down for, whether there would ever be an effective vaccine and whether the world could ever recover. Politicians made speeches that gave little indication about what the future would look like and, if anything, it was significantly more irritating when they tried to strike a hopeful tone. Micheál Martin would stand behind a lectern and quote Seamus Heaney, talking about *if we winter this one out, we can summer anywhere*. Personally, I always felt a little more 'Mid-Term Break' about the whole thing. Just put me in the 4-foot box and let's get this over with.

It had always struck me as odd that rotating taoisigh Micheál Martin and Leo Varadkar both seemed to find their inner poet during that period, and I always felt they should have kept up the charade. Like, if we were to ask Micheál Martin today, seeing how he's taoiseach again, if the government is going to hit its housing target for the year, he could say something like, 'To quote Seamus Heaney: no.'

The unseasonal warmth of that April and May felt like an

olive branch offered by God in exchange for the worst plague in living memory and, while we accepted it gratefully, the mood of the country remained fearful, shellshocked, wrong-footed entirely. Every night I would go to sleep telling myself that tomorrow would be different, just not in any way that mattered. In those first few numb months, sleep stopped being a hobby. Instead, it became just another block of time on an unchanging daily itinerary.

Perhaps inspired by my burgeoning talent for *Catan*, I delved further into the world of video games. Ignoring the responsibilities of my job as a digital journalist at a popular online publication pretty much entirely by that point, I spent most of my waking hours hanging out with my neighbours on *Animal Crossing: New Horizons*, which had come out towards the end of Covid's first April. *Animal Crossing* is unambiguously a game for children, with a Pan-European Game Information rating of being suitable for those aged three and up. The premise of the game is that you've just moved to an otherwise uninhabited island and purchased a property from a creature called Tom Nook (officially, he is a raccoon). Just like in the real world, Tom Nook makes you take out a mortgage (and, just like the real world, you have to top up the mortgage if you ever want to pursue any home improvements). Your debt to Tom Nook means that you have to set about completing a bunch of mundane life-admin tasks, such as digging for gold and foraging for items like seashells that you can sell to the general store (owned by Tom Nook's children, by the way). You cannot kill Tom Nook or his children, or even lightly threaten them. Or, if you can, then I never made it that far into the game.

In the game, you can also keep yourself afloat by finding rare fossils and capturing rare animals with your Outdoorsy Shovel, your Outdoorsy Fishing Rod and your Outdoorsy Net, and sell those rare specimens for a major profit, though God only knows if you're getting a good price from those Nook boys. They're the only game in town, though.

The good news is that the store sells clothes in a range of styles, so if you want to make your little guy look like a pirate or Spike Lee or something, you can. You've also got to deal with your 'neighbours', a cast of overly familiar animals who move to your island and try to talk to you and give you gifts. One of my neighbours was a ram in clown makeup named Pietro, who lived in a house that seemed to be entirely empty besides a workbench in the centre of one room with blue walls and heavenly white clouds. Just like real life.

There were other phases and rituals that kept me going during that time. My brother and I managed to kill at least a week and a half by playing darts in my bedroom over and over again until we got bored like children at 4 p.m. on Christmas Day. My parents had recently got our family's first dog, a King Charles cavalier named Arya – I guess it hadn't quite sunk in with us yet just how bad the ending of *Game of Thrones* really was. Arya shares a complexion with a McDonald's caramel sundae, and while she has since become the glue that holds our family together, at the time she was a mysterious presence. She learned how to be a dog in those early lockdown months, which is to say she never learned how to be a dog. Individually, each of us will complain that she has been spoiled, none of us quite prepared to take responsibility for our part in the spoiling. My father would almost certainly lay the blame at my mother's feet, but I have seen video footage of that man feeding Arya with a spoon. While she has grown to at least tolerate other dogs, she continues to believe she is a human baby, enjoys being picked up and carried, and has no sense of personal boundaries when it comes to the licking of a guest's face.

Arya's favourite pastime is chasing squirrels while she's out on her lead. Once while walking her, I had the sobering realisation that she chases the squirrels because she believes one day she will catch a squirrel, whereas I, holding her lead, know that she never actually will. It took no time at all for me to apply this principle to my own life, my ambitions, my squirrels, and to realise that no matter how fast I run, I too will only catch my squirrels if fate wills it, and I do not know who is holding my lead. Is it me? Oh God, it's me, isn't it?

I became increasingly spooked as it became increasingly clear that Covid was about to arrest professional progress for anyone who wasn't a front-facing-camera online comedian or a professional conspiracy grifter. I began to obsess over my age, feeling like a loser for having achieved so little by the age of twenty-seven. I was living under my parents' roof once again, fatally pessimistic about my prospects of ever owning a home or being normal enough to have a relationship. Certainly adrift in terms of my creative ambitions.

I whiled away the hours, sickening and stunning myself by intently researching the ages at which great artists had produced great art – or, indeed, the age at which mediocre artists produced mediocre art. It didn't really matter whether the art was good or bad, the common trend among the people who produced art, whether music or film or literature, was that they were for the most part on a clear trajectory towards eventual fulfilment of their goals by the age of twenty-seven. John Lennon, for example, wrote 'In My Life' at twenty-five. Roland Orzabal wrote 'Mad World' at nineteen. By the time The Notorious B.I.G. was the age I was then, he'd already been dead for three years. It was an utterly pointless exercise, predicated on a logic rife with holes, but that didn't stop me from letting it crush me.

I would find my favourite TV shows and scroll their cast lists on Wikipedia, taking a note of their ages, entering them into Google and dividing by *n* to get the average, desperately trying to convince myself that there was still time for me to do something. Did I want to be on television? Beyond a brief stint as John Proctor for my speech and drama class at a feis (which we *won*, by the way), I had no acting experience. The thought of being on camera made me want to stick my head in a guillotine, and even if I kept this stupid thing on my shoulders, getting up early to film would have been the death of me.

Still, I tormented myself over the very idea that actors, sports stars, pop stars were younger than me. I don't think I wanted to be any of those things, but evidently there was an active dissatisfaction with my present trajectory taking root and gnarling hard. Did you know that Lauryn Hill was only twenty-two when she made *The Miseducation of Lauryn Hill*? How is that even possible? Wondering if my younger self had been any closer to artistic realisation, I began rifling through the notebooks I'd kept as a teenager. Mostly what I found were some unreadable attempts at literature featuring teenage male protagonists who, if I met them as a grown man, I would have given a clip around the ear. Besides that, there was song after song after song of lyrics that read like

My Chemical Romance fanfiction. It was certainly a mercy that I had not stumbled into any sort of public success in my early life, because my output was truly abominable. So poor that I began to question whether I'd ever had any talent in the first place.

By 2020, I'd become sufficiently established in Irish media that the publication I worked for gave me enough breathing space to write opinion columns several times a week in amongst reporting the news (by which I mean car crashes, the weather and Covid numbers). It gave me the opportunity to channel my many frustrations regarding the order of Irish society from the top down, with a primary focus on the inaction of our government on the matters of housing and homelessness. As you can see, my words made an enormous difference. Really, the job boiled down to me giving two fingers to any public figure who said or did anything I didn't like. It's a pretty nice way to earn a living but, even at the age of twenty-seven, living at home with very few overheads, it wasn't all that much of a living.

Between resenting the job I'd been doing for four of the previous five years and realising that a pixellated raccoon had me by the balls since I'd put that second storey on my house, I started to fall asleep not only as a means of escape but a means of protest. *You can't get me in there, Tom Nook, you landlord scum.* I would sleep for most of my nine-to-five hours and had little or no trouble sleeping when it came time to sleep for real, during the hours that everybody else was also sleeping. Eventually, even sleep wasn't enough, and I took my savings and a credit-union loan, which I thought was a good idea for some reason, and I quit my job.

At the time, it was my intention to retire from journalism entirely. I had grown exhausted of a job that beckoned me to immerse myself in the pollution of algorithmic media, having my brain pulled in a thousand different directions in the name of knowing what was happening in the news. I don't remember doing very much work at all between March and August, when I finally managed to quit. At least part of this was on principle. Covid, and some bad decisions that were well-covered in the media at the time, had resulted in my employer cutting salaries across the board. My own salary was cut by 25 per cent, and I had resolved to commensurately increase my daytime sleeping. This way, I reasoned, at least my real wages would remain roughly the same.

After I quit, I went to Westport for two weeks with some friends, luxuriating in the golden sunsets at the seemingly endless succession of golden beaches they've got over there, conscientiously leaving the local pubs by 8 p.m. in accordance with the laws of that period, climbing Croagh Patrick, watching the extended editions of the *Lord of the Rings* movies on rainy days – and accidentally getting the highest I've ever been in my life.

On our last day in the town, we decided to make some edibles from a bag of weed we'd brought from Dublin. We didn't have a weighing scale, so two of our sharper-eyed members decided to eyeball it, and disaster ensued. Halfway through *World War Z*, a movie I do not remember a minute of besides that it's about a zombie apocalypse and heavily features Israel for some reason – I mean, seriously, we're talking one of the worst movies you could possibly watch while high – the edibles began to take effect. As we sat in silence and watched this upsettingly unmemorable movie play out, it became clear that the room was suffering.

'I have consumed substances,' one of my friends announced definitively after about two hours of total silence, saying what we were all thinking. Before the movie had even ended, another decamped to his bedroom and, at some point between then and the time I went to bed, he texted me to tell me that he was scared he'd given himself Parkinson's.

Three of us were now left in the room, a typical Irish grandmother's living room with thin floral-print carpet and old wallpaper gone spongy to the touch. There were heavy cabinets, presses and tables. Old wood, good wood. There was no picture of John F. Kennedy on the wall, but there might as well have been. Stupefied though we were, one of us managed to fumble with the laptop connected to the TV via a HDMI cable to put on some old episodes of *Jeopardy!* from before Alex Trebek died. We were too fucked to even make the 'pew pew' noises on the Daily Double. We watched somewhere in the region of a dozen episodes, not one of us venturing an answer to a single question. Eventually, we clawed our way to bed, leaving one friend to stay up and let in the final member of our cohort, who had spent the day not doing drugs at all but instead embarking on twelve-hour hike around Mayo. When he got back, he asked the last man standing if we'd intended to get that high. *No, no we did not.*

I'd been sharing a bedroom with another member of the crew, a small room with two single beds and a sink, arranged in such a way that the door couldn't close. The morning after this ill-fated escapade, we were packing up our things and preparing for a train ride across the country all the way back to Heuston. Our checkout time was 11 a.m., as is standard, and at roughly 10.45 I realised it was time for me to vomit. With the house's only bathroom occupied, I ingeniously remembered the sink in the corner of our room. I rushed there to relieve the burning pressure in my stomach, rectifying the many wrongs of the previous twenty-four hours. I vomited fulsomely into the small pan-shaped sink, and then lifted the lever on the tap to wash away these sins and put it all behind me, forever. Had to have been 10.48 a.m. by then. 10.49 a.m.

Ten minutes to checkout. I lifted the lever on the tap, and no water came out.

'Hey,' I gurgled into the hall. 'Do you know if this sink works?'

'Uh, I don't know, man,' my friend called back. It didn't.

The relief I felt at being unburdened of whatever poison had been eating my body from the inside was suddenly tempered by the realisation that it was suddenly my responsibility to fetch a drinking glass to serve as the instrument of my martyrdom, to be scooped unto by mine own hands, and filled with vomit, and brought to the kitchen, and rinsed, and the process be repeated thus and so until the vomit was diluted enough to be washed away and wiped away with water and hand soap and toilet paper. Mercifully, the owner of the accommodation did not turn up until a little while after the official checkout time, and so my shame was never discovered. Between then and the train home, I wandered off and found a big tree to sit underneath. It is events like this that can contribute to one's self-perception as being fundamentally unserious. It is a dangerous thing, I think, to decide that your life is supposed to matter.

Truly unemployed for the first time since I was eighteen, I moved into a spare room in my friend Adam's apartment on the Old Kent Road in London at the start of 2021. Adam had been my best friend as a teenager, and possesses the closest thing I've ever seen to a legitimate photographic memory. In our early twenties, he had dropped out of a maths degree in Trinity College to become a cocktail barman in London, where he had transformed from a sub-60-kilogram maths nerd to a sub-60-kilogram keg-hauling, moustache-wearing, cocktail-shaker-shaking dynamo. He'd been made redundant during the first lockdown after seven years on the job and got himself a bumper payout.

For the first few months of my stay on the Old Kent Road, Adam and I mostly slept in, played the mystery-ball mode on FIFA and made cocktails. Well, Adam made cocktails. I provided the company. Somewhere in between our scheduled activities I found the time to write the guts of a novel, which is what I was nominally taking time away from work to do, and the rest of the time I slept. Granted, some Saturdays I'd make the journey to Kilburn to get fucked up with some friends who lived out there, but that was always preceded and followed by some of the most intense and intentional sleeping you've ever seen in your life.

My room on the Old Kent Road was huge. It fit a queen-sized bed in one corner and a futon in the other corner facing the door, as well as a desk from IKEA that I assembled with my own bare hands after dragging it back on the 188 from Greenwich. It overlooked what has to be one of the loudest roads in the entirety of Zone 2, but it was well-connected by buses and living on a high street guarantees you access to the kind of Cypriot-Turkish cuisine that others can only dream of. The London summer was loud and hot and I stayed up late, writing and binge-watching *Naruto*, or taking prescription painkillers and reading *Lonesome Dove* by Larry McMurtry to myself in the closest thing I can do to a Matthew McConaughey impersonation. For a very brief period, I tried drinking alone, mixing lime cordial with vodka, blasting out tweets and sleeping. Unfortunately, either the lime cordial or the vodka or the combination of both left my oesophagus stuck in some sort of hiccup samsara and I realised that drinking alone wasn't for me either.

I knew I would need a job eventually, and I was searching. Don't ask me how exactly, but I made it to the third round of interviews for a £60,000-a-year position at BNP Paribas. For the life of me I can't imagine what role, with my five years' experience of offering my opinion on Leo Varadkar and Ryan Tubridy, I could possibly have been qualified for. Obviously, they came to the same conclusion in the end.

A series of interviews for the Macmillan cancer charity also ended in disappointment and, feeling defeated, I began to sink deeper into sleep. The worst part is that I'd bought a suit jacket, a shirt and a range of ties for these interviews, ties for which I should have been reimbursed. *Just because I don't work for you doesn't mean this wasn't a work expense on your behalf, you charlatan.*

I applied to be a copywriter at Victoria's Secret, at Disney, at every fintech startup with more money than sense. If I was lucky, I'd get an email back about three months after applying, telling me they wouldn't be proceeding with my application. It was a sobering thought. That my years of excoriating think pieces and mildly funny tweets about Irish culture had left me unqualified to do virtually anything besides the very thing I was trying to get away from. And yet, if I wanted to change career, there seemed to be nowhere to start but the bottom, and the thought of working for someone else, to someone else's schedule, all for a minimum wage-ish salary, was unthinkable to me. So I slept again, and I enjoyed it every time.

The rent on the Old Kent Road flat was probably the most reasonable I've ever paid in my life, though I happen to know it has gone up since. Still, I was rapidly running out of money, and was beginning to wonder if I was unemployable. Against this backdrop, I found it surprisingly easy to be blissful, which is certainly not my default state. A strange phenomenon had started to occur in the mornings when I woke up. With my eyes closed and my body turned half on its side, positioned, as one partner once described it, like I'm 'guarding something', I would regard the pale-yellow sensation of morning rebounding off the cream-coloured walls and through my eyelids. Starting from my feet and emanating upwards like convection currents was a sensation of euphoria, a feeling of relaxation as though my body had never even known tension. It was a feeling that caught me off-guard without shocking me. I was too relaxed to be shocked. It was especially confusing given that my feet had been causing me all sorts of grief for the past few years, fallen arches leading to shin splints leading to lower back pain leading to weight gain leading to more sleep.

Part of me wondered if I'd crossed some kind of physical threshold and accessed a cycle of sleep that opened the floodgates for all the body's endogenous morphine. The feeling was less than a shimmer, less than a buzz, just a pleasing awareness of sensation. My brain had slipped into low-battery mode. Or, more seriously yet, battery-preservation mode. Advanced settings. Lights down to zero. Volume zero. No transmission, in or out. No connectivity. Everything had been switched off besides the most basic, vital functions – whichever internal apps kept me breathing and stopped me from pissing myself. Warm butter ran through my veins, and the tips of my fingers tingled with a sense of relief. *Is this what it means to relax?* It had taken me twenty-eight years to realise that there was a difference between relaxing and feeling incredibly tense while lying as still as possible or sitting on a couch. As it turned out, I had only ever been any good at the latter.

The feeling travelled through my body, bringing with it a sense of healing and restoration that I knew was temporary, that I knew would only last while I remained here, in bed, consciously making sure not to do anything foolish like curl my toes or rotate my angle or anything else that might scare the feeling away. I've never known what it means to 'find one's centre' or even what discipline that phrase comes from – yoga? Martial arts? – but I think that's what I was doing. On days when I did it right, the euphoria would reach my spine and I would soak in pleasure, only just awake enough to register how good I felt. How was I supposed to get up? Why should I be expected to interrupt this feeling? Why would I voluntarily bring this to an end?

I guess when people hear how much you like to sleep they probably think you've got some kind of problem that you're hiding from. That's probably what I would think if somebody told me they slept as much as I sleep. That seems like a fair call. And let's call a spade a spade, that's almost certainly what was happening here.

I struggle with the real world. The physical world. The corporeal realm. Whatever way you want to think about it. I don't struggle with it outwardly. I move across it fine, though my legs are sore and my toes go numb and sometimes I taste blood in my mouth when I try to run. My friends and family would tell you that I have a low threshold for pain. I don't believe that's true. I think it's much more likely that I have a chronic pain condition that I can't bring myself to do anything about because it's simply too much of a drag to summon the energy.

I know they say that the desire to sleep all of the time can be a sign of depression, so maybe I'm depressed, but I don't entirely buy it. I know that not only are there those who struggle with the physicality of this world more than I do, but that I am, in fact, among the luckiest people to have existed in the history of humanity. This is not to say that people like me or people in general have it easy. I believe that the number of people burdened with the human condition who find it easy must be vanishingly small, but I am conscious that of the billions upon billions of people who have walked this earth, I am undoubtedly in the 0.00001 percentile for being a total pussy.

I guess I was in my late twenties or early thirties when I first heard the phrase 'social battery'. Whatever age I was, I'd reached the point where new phrases for concepts that have always existed rub me the wrong way no matter how evocative or applicable they are. And I can picture my social battery very clearly, split open, wounds scabbed over with a corrosive crust, the Energizer Bunny lying dead in the distance behind it. I have tried to eat bananas and granola in the morning. I've cut out alcohol for months at a time. Hell, there have been times in my life when I ran 10 kilometres several times a week and got my time down to forty-five minutes. None of it seems to make me feel any more enthusiastic about leaving my bed. It seems to be the Nietzschean 'will to power' in conflict with the Knoxvillian 'will to annihilate oneself totally'. Perhaps the two impulses are one and the same. After all, if you gave me the option of what I truly want to do with my time, I'd be asleep before we'd even shaken on the deal.

I've always been struck by how people toss around the old adage that Eskaleut languages have however many words for snow, as if this phenomenon doesn't have immediate parallels in virtually every other language, including Hiberno-English. But it doesn't snow here. Here we're used to the rain, so we have a range of words to specify the quality of rain we might be experiencing. 'Lashing', for example, usually carries the suggestion of a wild and heavy rain, though it can also be used to convey the idea that the rain is simply too heavy for going out in. 'Drizzle' is perhaps the most common species of rain we encounter in Ireland, light enough to almost be ambient, rain so light that you can spend all day in it and only fully realise it when you get home and notice that your outerwear is nearly soaked through.

Beyond Hiberno-English, the same thing seems to apply to sleep. We have different words for sleeping depending on the time of day, the duration, the depth. Snoozing, for example, denotes a carefree sleep. Nobody snoozes in a hospital room armchair. Nobody is catching some Zs or getting their forty winks while they're waiting for bad news. Between 'snoozing', 'drowsing', 'dozing' and 'napping', most of our words for sleep seem to contain within them a suggestion of lightness. We have fewer words for deep sleep, though the few we have are powerful. The connotations of 'slumber' are unmistakable. It's the kind of word that should be reserved for an enormous fictional dragon who's been sleeping on top of a pile of gold for a thousand years, and ideally would only come at the end of the sentence 'Who disturbs my—?'

There is, however, no specific word for the kind of sleep I seem to rely upon. Recreational sleep, sleep as a hobby, sleep as a means of avoidance. I snooze, I doze, I nap, and on rare and blissful occasions I find a way to truly slumber. None of these words seem to appropriately encapsulate the specific kind of sleep I indulge in most.

I believe the high that I am chasing requires more than simply a good night of sleep and a guaranteed lie-in. Mere minutes separate the morning of a bank holiday Monday and a regular old Tuesday, and I count each minute without even trying. In order to rediscover the euphoria I once felt in London, I think I would need to offer my body at least three months of blank white squares on a calendar. No work, no responsibilities, no demands. An indulgent and impossible idea. Incompatible with all the demands of my life: paying rent, earning a living, meeting new people, falling in love, making myself a better person and the world a better place. All things that you can't do while you're sleeping.

I know it's not very 'what will you do with your one wild and precious life?' of me. Sorry, Mary Oliver. I'm blowing it, is that what you want to hear? I am screwing this thing up six ways from Sunday, Mary. You can bring Wendy Cope in here too, or the guy who wrote that one about the plums in the icebox, and you can read me all the life-affirming poems you like. I can already feel myself falling asleep in protest.

It Occurs To You

IT WAS THE summer I'd finished my undergraduate degree when it occurred to me that I might have cancer.

It's essential to understand from the get-go that I did not have cancer. Everyone around me knew that I didn't have cancer. Friends, family and, eventually, doctors all made it clear to me that I had no reason to suspect that I was even sick. If you'd known me then, you'd have told me the very same thing. This is not a suspenseful story. Not a story about hospital waiting rooms or waiting for biopsy results. Those things are part of the story, but this isn't a story about being sick. At least not in the way I thought I was. In moments of self-loathing, I worry it's a story that could be read as little

189

more than an insult to those who have lived with or died from cancer, or seen loved ones go through the very same. Which is to say just about everyone. It's a story that at first might seem self-indulgent, and it is undoubtedly indulgent, just of something much darker than the self.

It is the story of how I ended up believing I had cancer – 'believing' I had cancer the same way that you 'believe' yourself to be reading these words right now. I was certain of it.

One evening that summer, I was just over halfway through running the suburban 5-kilometre route I'd plotted out for myself in a bid to lose the weight I'd piled on having spent roughly three months on my back in a single bed in Trinity College's Botany Bay writing my thesis: 'Is Consciousness Causal? A Critical Evaluation of the Claim that Consciousness is Epiphenomenal'.

The 10,000-word dissertation was a study in neuroethics – which is a real discipline and not just something I made up – examining whether human behaviour can be caused by conscious thought processes or whether conscious thought processes themselves are the result of the imperceptible movement of neurons in the brain that takes place entirely without our conscious input. At the time, it was the longest project I'd ever worked on, about four times longer than any other college assignment. It was also 33.3 per cent of the entire grade for my degree.

The idea for the paper had come to me one day in the hangar of Heuston Station, pigeons ambling about my feet as I stood in front of the vending machine to buy a bottle of Coke. As I punched 'E4' into the keypad, I wondered why I'd chosen that combination of letters and numbers, when traps A4 to D4 would have also served me a Coke just the same. You could say that I chose E4 because I grew up watching *Scrubs* and *Friends*. But why not A4? I'd been writing on A4 paper my whole life, making jokes about D4 accents, reading Wikipedia pages about the damage C4 can do. But let me move the story along B4 I start to bore you.

Coming up with confabulations as to why I may have chosen E4 rather than another combination of buttons on the keypad is beside the point. I knew that truth. It was clear to me that the matter had been decided unconsciously. That is to say, without my conscious input. Quite quickly, I began to notice all the many nearly automated behaviours I, and we as a species, execute from day to day. We think of ourselves – our conscious selves, the layer of ourselves that reasons and deliberates and ratiocinates – as in control of the choices we make. It's pretty much the guiding principle of free will as an idea. That there is some kind of internal, immeasurable

X-factor that grants us control over the neuronal movement necessary to reason and decide and act. Does that make sense? Does it make sense for us to believe that we are in possession of some non-physical quality, such as a soul, that causes physical effects, such as behaviours, to take place? Wouldn't it make more sense, on a physical level, to think of our thoughts, and our motivations and our impulses and, therefore, our behaviours, as being governed by the same physical principles that govern everything else? That there is matter on a subatomic level – the 86 billion neurons in our brains – jumping around, setting in motion inalterable chains of events that we don't become aware of until it's too late? Until you've already fallen in love, until you've already poured salt into your coffee instead of sugar, until you've made up your mind that you must have cancer.

After all, there was no conscious activity that day that prompted me – a boy of twenty-two, with no family history of the disease – to stop dead as I passed Ballyboden GAA club while in the middle of a run, in the golden hour of an August evening. To pull out my smartphone and google *bowel cancer young person?*. What was it about that moment, a time in my life when all was externally well, that primed me not only to make this enquiry, but to be so captivated by the results as to believe myself marked for death?

Sweat and melted hair gel stung my eyes as I turned up the brightness on my phone's cracked screen to read a tabloid article about a British man in his late thirties who had died of bowel cancer after having his concerns dismissed by doctor after doctor. The red-top reporting naturally made it sound like these doctors had done little more than point and laugh when this poor man came in to tell them he'd been shitting blood, and even after just a few weeks as something approximating a journalist I knew better than to trust that the reporting contained all the relevant details. I knew, too, that it was probably not prudent to decide I was dying based on anecdotal evidence that some man, somewhere, had also once died. Surely, I had always known that it was statistically possible for people under the age of fifty-five to be diagnosed with and even die of bowel cancer. Surely, this was not new information to me. And yet reading this article prompted a seismic shift in my thinking, entire tectonic plates of baseless anxieties dry-humping one another and causing the fault lines along the grooves of my brain to split open and drown my mind in crude oil.

It feels wrong that anybody's life should turn upon an event so frivolous as to barely register as an event at all. Anyone looking at me in the moment my run slowed to a crawl and I tapped the words into my phone and read as

I walked would not have known that they were watching a young man about to flush six months of his life down the toilet. What should have been a fleeting thought came instead like a harpoon fired from some place I couldn't see, spearing through my side like I'd collided with a door handle.

I don't believe that I consciously willed the thought into being. Whatever activity had been happening on the conscious plane of my mind had been far more proximal. I had been thinking about running. I'd been thinking about the internship I'd started a few weeks earlier. I'd been thinking about what I was going to do with the rest of my life. And then, between one stride and the next, it had occurred to me that I was dying.

I didn't think it up, the thought didn't come as a well-reasoned conclusion to a series of other premises that I'd been stacking one on top of another like a sturdy Connemara wall. No, this was just something that occurred to me, the same way that some mornings it occurs to you that you'd like an iced latte rather than your usual coffee order. It's not because you weighed the pros and cons of either, but because your body has some impulse and you follow it, because it's your body and your body makes the rules – beaming instructions onto the JCDecaux billboard of consciousness, the steel rigging and canvas and printer ink that we think of as the 'self'.

This seems like an accurate way to describe what's going on inside our heads, doesn't it? It's not as if we're in there ourselves, forging the thoughts from wet clay. The urge to google scary stories about an illness didn't emerge from what I think of as my personality, this surface collection of attributes that forms the conversations and interactions I have with myself and with others, but from somewhere uncharted and abyssal. It has long occurred to me that 'it occurred to me' might be the most underused phrase in the English language – a flaw that is at least in some way addressed by the Irish language. We don't say, 'I am sad.' We say, '*Tá brón orm.*' (There is sorrow upon me.) The 'sorrow' and the 'me' are not one and the same, they are definitionally separate. The feeling is something that happens to the self, not something that the self summons into the world.

All it had really taken was for me to think about a certain kind of cancer in a moment when – entirely unbeknownst to me – my mind was a fertile spot for the development of a good old-fashioned delusion. Something shifted immediately in the core of my being – the opposite of love at first sight. Everything about it made sense to me. There was a rapidness to everything from then on. I began behaving, from the moment I got back to my front door having trudged the rest of my route, as though I truly believed I had cancer. I didn't have any symptoms, per se. My stomach had always bothered me, that was pretty much the long and short of the diagnostic criteria that, obviously, I felt I met. I counted on my hands the lifestyle factors that may have contributed. Choices I'd made and been making in my young life for which I was now apparently and deservedly paying the price. I'd eaten too much red meat, I'd drunk too much high-fructose corn syrup, I hadn't eaten enough vegetables.

Colon cancer was the perfect disease to appeal to whatever avaricious spirit had taken the reins of my mind. Fast-acting and often symptomless until it's too late. It was as though the thought had infiltrated my mind and installed a puppet regime to run things while the version of me that existed before the delusion took hold was little more than a government-in-exile, trying vainly to rally the parts of my brain that were still loyal to my actual wellbeing.

I told my mother I was worried about it and she did what she could to assuage me, though she was obviously taken aback by how sincerely I believed that I was dying. We made an appointment with the GP.

As the days went by and I waited for the consultation, I was sure that I could feel the corruption growing in my left side. Not only that, but I could feel it metastasise. I could feel it in my lungs or my brain or my pancreas. Wherever it would be most fatal, most irreversible. I could feel it develop. Just days before it had been stage 2, and there had still been time to save me. But by now it was stage 3, stage 4. Too little, too late.

Within forty-eight hours of my mid-run epiphany, I had stopped eating pretty much entirely – I'd decided that my years of consuming whatever I liked had been little more than hubris and now the gods were taking their pound of flesh. In the weeks that followed, every moment was infected by the fear that I was dying. I did sit-ups in the work bathroom to see if it would have some kind of tellingly adverse effect. (What was I expecting to happen? That I would explode?) In a bid to increase my fibre intake, I bought tubs of celery and ate them raw sitting on a bench in St Kevin's churchyard down Camden Row. I wrote a poem about dying and I performed it at an open-mic night. I sought the advice of just about every friend I had, driving all of them demented as I asked them about their diets, their bowel movements, how they could be so sure I wasn't dying. In short, I made the whole thing everyone else's problem.

To take further stock of my life at that time, I had recently begun an internship at JOE.ie, a website that was more or less the Irish take on Buzzfeed. Its tagline at the time was 'The Voice of Irish Men', which had always made me laugh. That's me, alright. In my job interview, I suggested that they change the slogan and they eventually did, opting for 'The Voice of Irish People at Home and Abroad', which is tautological, but I guess I was probably pretty checked out by the time they made the change and, either way, it was better than hanging a 'Boy's Only Clubhouse' sign on the door.

At this stage of my career, my tasks included endeavours such as eating the world's hottest chili pepper on camera as part of a campaign run by Tesco, and interviewing cultural bastions at the peak of their relevance, like the bassist from Stereophonics and one of the guys from The Prodigy who wasn't Keith Flint or Maxim. God only knows what I managed to ask them, especially as I was managing the realisation that I had such a slim chance of surviving past Christmas.

Until it had occurred to me that I was dying, I suppose I'd been relatively happy with how things were going. It seemed to me that I'd gained a foothold in the famously nepotistic Irish-media landscape, and I'd found an employer who didn't seem to mind that I spent half of my day on Twitter telling everyone else in Irish media how shit they were. The compensation for those first six months was more of a stipend than a salary, naturally, but what did I need money for anyway? Either I was dying or I was losing my mind.

By no means did I love my job, but the job was, at its core, all about writing. While I've dreamed of being many things, writing is the only way of making a living that has ever struck me as plausible, needing as I do to hide behind something, a mechanism that mediates between me and any Other, a buffer that keeps me out of the physical world as much as possible. Writing is that. It's why I was drawn to it then and why I'm drawn to it now.

Soon after my epiphany, though, I began to struggle at work. I'd wake up with ice coursing through my veins, like a bowling ball had been dropped on my belly, every minute movement feeling as though I was stepping into a river of television static. When I explained what was going on to my boss, I didn't even have the decency to imply that I may have been suffering from a delusion, only that I appeared to have some digestive disease and that I was getting it checked out. 'Maybe Crohn's,' I said, realising that *I think I have cancer and I have no evidence to support that claim* might in some way curtail or otherwise negatively affect this burgeoning career in multimedia journalism-cum-content aggregation. To his credit, he was really nice about it.

It was a confusing time. I woke up every morning of that first week feeling as though I was standing between two trains hurtling past one another, as though I was one last supervillain crank away from being lowered into a vat of acid. I thought I was dying. I should have known I wasn't, but I didn't.

It may already be clear to you that I possess precisely none of the virtue referred to by many as 'stoicism'. I have no capacity whatsoever to keep my concerns to myself. If I believe I'm in danger, then, buddy, you're going to hear about it. And I *always* believe I'm in danger. I'm not proud of this, but it's my firm belief that few people who see themselves as stoics have all that much to be proud of either. Real stoics don't know that they're stoics. They're too busy actually getting on with it to go around telling everyone how much they're enduring and how we should all learn to be a little more like them. The world is full, maybe more full than ever, of self-styled stoics whose self-styled stoicism seemingly does not a whit to prevent them from being driven to distraction by how others feel and think and behave. If you were a real stoic, my whining wouldn't bother you so much.

Whatever day I'd taken off work to go to the doctor coincided with my usual guy being out of town, so I ended up seeing a locum first. I was given a lift, parasite that I am, to the doctor's office by my aunt and godmother Collette.

She was quiet and sympathetic throughout the journey. I suppose she'd been at least partially informed by my mother about whatever the hell was going on with me. I sat there, embarrassed, not sure exactly what to say. *Hi, Collette, thanks for the lift, either I am dying or I'm losing my mind.*

The consultation with the locum, a stern and thin man of seemingly Germanic provenance, was brief. I laid out my concerns, and he told me that nothing I was describing would raise alarm bells for bowel cancer in someone so young. Despite the tabloid headlines I'd seen and statistical outliers I'd collected through hours of painstaking online research, I felt as though arguing was not the right course of action. We mostly discussed diet, and he perfunctorily inserted one latexed finger into my ass, just in case, I guess. *Cool. Great. So that's what that feels like.*

So I'd been advised that it was very unlikely that I had cancer of the bowel or rectum, which is exactly what happened to the guy in the first article I'd read. Textbook. While I did what I could to communicate my distress, I was conscious that to show too much certainty would look a little ludicrous. I held back. Feigned reassurance. He seemed to have little interest in whatever was behind my hypochondria (which, these days, they call 'health anxiety', in case you hadn't heard). For my €60 I got little more than a suggestion that I eat more aubergines, which I said I'd do, knowing even as I said it that it was a lie. Starving or subsisting solely on celery or raisins or some other pleasureless chewable was one thing, but apparently aubergine is where I draw the line. I left the doctor's office as queasy as I'd been when I entered and I pretended for the sake of my godmother, who had waited to drop me home again, that I'd been satisfied with the outcome. Knowing that I would never wake up happy again until I'd been colonoscopised, I got through the front door at home and immediately made another appointment for the following week.

I returned to the clinic when the locum had departed and my usual GP had returned. Finally, a real doctor, not some fair-weather blow-in. Surely this man would see sense. He would take one look at me and realise that I had, at most, six months left to live. How could he deny it?

It had now been two or three weeks since I'd first realised I was dying and, by that point, I was struggling to stand up straight due to what was surely a sizeable malignant mass in my left flank — and certainly not pain that had begun to develop as a resultant combination of psychosomatic anxiety and me cultivating the diet of a wild rabbit. I was doubled over, drawn in from the centre, collapsing in on myself like lawn furniture. The doctor would be able to see it. He'd give me a 'World's Bravest and Most Righteous Martyr' lollipop, and that would teach everyone a lesson for doubting me, and then I'd die. That would show them.

The doctor in question was the father of a former secondary-school classmate of mine, which did give me some degree of apprehension before turning up with my baseless claim that I had cancer of the bowel, but I'd been left with no choice. Enough time had already been wasted. I needed to start treatment.

I weighed 65 kilograms by this point. Not underweight just yet, but a full 8 kilograms lighter than I'd been when the fear had begun just weeks earlier. And let me tell you, I hadn't been back out on a run since. Weight loss is a common symptom of bowel cancer. It's also a common symptom of starving yourself because you think you've got bowel cancer, but I found that line of argument terribly unconvincing. Put Occam's razor back in the drawer, I just found a pair of scissors and I am going for a run.

My doctor, who had been my GP for a long time and whom I had been brought to as a young teenager when in the midst of a particularly persistent bout of sadness, was an understanding guy. Balding and mousy and thorough and intense. Leaning across the desk and finishing every sentence with 'Okay?' like he was making sure he had my full cooperation in everything he explained. What he explained was that I very probably did not have that kind of cancer because there was no reason to suspect that I had the kind of cancer. I was too young, I had no family history of the disease, I had no meaningful symptoms.

But by then I'd spent more than enough time torturing myself on WebMD and Cancer Research UK and the CDC stats pages, running my cursor over all the 'Incidents by Age' graphs, taking brief respite upon seeing cases of bowel cancer fall to near zero when you go under the age of thirty-five. But near zero is not zero. Somebody has to get it, and that somebody was me.

I can recall much of my research. The most up-to-date statistics from the time showed that there were around 3,000 cases of bowel cancer in Ireland per year. Around 90 per cent of those occurred in people over fifty, with most of the remainder occurring in people between forty and fifty. But there are always anomalies, and I'd found plenty of tabloids reporting sensationally about studies they certainly didn't understand but that seemed to suggest that bowel cancer is becoming more common in young people. Why wouldn't I be at the vanguard of this burgeoning new class?

On at least one occasion, I had actually walked straight out of the JOE.ie office in the middle of my shift in order to call the Irish Cancer Society, wasting their time as if they could heal me over the phone. As though they could tell me, once and for all, that, no, I didn't have cancer. Which of course was basically what they said. Or at least that it would be something close to unheard of for a twenty-two-year-old with no genetic predisposition for bowel cancer and no real symptoms to have – and die from – bowel cancer. I kept the woman, whose voice I don't recall, on the line long enough to reassure me a few more times and eventually accepted I'd have to let her move on to the people out there who were, you know, actually sick.

Coping mechanisms like this one were good for ten, fifteen minutes of respite before the obsession returned and, with it, the compulsion to call a helpline, to browse cancer forums, to browse hypochondria forums, to try to find evidence of miracle recoveries, to plan my funeral, to find some source that would say something like *twenty-two-year-olds from Dublin with a freckle underneath their right eye actually can't get cancer. You did it, Carl!*

In that second consultation, this time with my *real* doctor and not some Johnny-come-blow-in, I was told that there is actually a name for this kind of behaviour. That sort of disordered mix of obsessions and compulsions taking over one's life. I don't remember exactly how he phrased it but it was something along the lines of: 'I don't think you have cancer. I think you have obsessive-compulsive disorder.'

I was indignant. I was insulted. I was apoplectic, in fact. *I'm over here dying of cancer and this shmuck with his fancy medical books thinks I've got the Michael J. Fox disease from* Scrubs? The Matchstick Men *disease? I'm not over here putting my books in order and washing my hands twenty times in a row, doc. This is real!*

As it turns out, OCD actually doesn't work or look like it does on TV or in the movies, but I wouldn't figure that out for at least another year.

At that appointment, it was my insistence that I be referred for a colonoscopy, even after the fulsome reassurance of two doctors, that eventually prompted my GP to gently suggest that I was losing my grip on reality.

I was not to be deterred.

Under duress, and with my mother present, the doctor referred me to a clinic in Lucan that would carry out the colonoscopy a few months down the line. Better than nothing, though of course I was certain I'd have passed the point of no return by then, if I hadn't already. Soon it would be my mother looking solemnly out from the CMYK ink of a tabloid front page, tearfully telling the world that her son – who had been wise enough to foresee his own death – was turned away by every doctor in Dublin and castigated as some kind of lunatic. I fantasised regularly about holding some kind of living funeral, where everyone could come to my hospital bed before I died and say nice things about me.

Even still, it managed to evade me almost entirely that I was fucking nuts.

I suppose as some kind of compromise, I agreed to at least try to take the minimum dose of Prozac, an antidepressant that is generally thought of as the first port of call for OCD. Blue-and-white plasticky capsules that stick in your throat like a bitch. As I'd feared, they upset my stomach, which is the last thing you need when you've convinced yourself you've got bowel cancer, so I packed them in after about three days and figured I'd never use them again.

This episode was not the first time I'd become preoccupied with my own death. I had started college in September 2010 and didn't turn eighteen until the following February. A few days before Freshers' Week kicked off my grandfather collapsed in St Agnes' church in Crumlin. He sang in the choir on Sundays, and he'd made the short walk to the church every day for the previous fifty years or so, one of his two daily pilgrimages. One to the church, and another to Brady's or Liddy's to pick up the *Evening Herald*.

He was eighty-nine at the time of his collapse, and the church was an old building in the middle of September. So, not so strange that a man might feel the heat and grow light-headed. Someone, some good Samaritan I suppose, brought him home to the council house where my mother was raised and, as luck would have it, I was there that day. An aunt of mine – does this essay make it sound like I spend all my time being driven places by my aunts? – had picked me up at Heuston Station on my way back from Kilkenny where my girlfriend at the time lived and had brought me to Crumlin to meet my mother, who had taken my nana to the credit union. In my teen years, my mother seemed permanently to be taking my nana to the credit union. *How much credit did she have?*

My grandfather and I spoke only briefly that day, me in the armchair where he usually sat to watch Manchester United or read *Ireland's Own*, him lying on the couch that I'd been using as a makeshift goal since I was old enough to walk and kick a ball. There was a tag sticking out of the couch that read 'By Order' on it, and when I was a child my grandfather used to scare me that if I kicked the ball against it too hard then 'Mr By Order' would come to the house and – I don't know – take me away, I guess? Kill me, possibly? That bit was always left to my imagination and I can tell you that, in my imagination, Mr By Order looked like an Orangeman, or at least like one of those guys from the Batchelors baked-beans ads. For the first few years of my life, I spent every day in my grandparents' house while my parents worked. Even as I got older, the amount of time I spent there didn't actually diminish by all that much. It was as much my home as my actual home.

I believe he always loved me very much. My grandfather that is, not that sadistic psycho Mr By Order. He used to take me to play pitch and putt and would scold me for all the Coke I'd drink. Once I found a bottle of Diet Coke in his own golf bag and I never let him hear the end of it. When I think of him now, it's of him regaling me with stories of his own football-playing days for St Francis. I don't remember what we discussed that day, and it doesn't matter to me. I consider it a great privilege that I got to see him one last time before he died in his sleep later that night.

I can't really imagine a better death than the one my grandfather got. Less than eighteen months later, my grandmother took a fall on Good Friday and broke some bone or other. A rib or a hip, certainly something important. She was eighty-six by then, and frail, having had a stent put into her heart only a few years earlier. Despite the creep of old age, she had remained a merciless card player and a wonderful conversationalist, a diligent lighter of candles at exam time, and her appetite for brandy and red lemonade was undiminished.

She rallied from the subsequent surgery miraculously, but fell victim to some kind of bug on the ward of St James's Hospital where she'd been convalescing. She died after six weeks of terrible pain, having been moved to her home in Crumlin where a cot was made up in the dining room, the room where we'd all spent so many Sunday evenings trying to get through the entire twenty-five rounds of Bonkers, a card game that very few people seem to have heard of outside of my family and, even as I write this, I cannot be certain that it is what you would call a 'real' game. After contracting the hospital bug, she was no longer able to get up or down the stairs, no longer able to stomach a single meal. My mother was at her side every day and, to hear her tell it, I'm not sure my nana could even speak. All of her grandchildren were kept well away as she died, which underscored to us all how bad the situation must have been. My father's mother would follow some months later, dying suddenly but not unexpectedly at a grand old age, a fate that seemed perfectly merciful in light of what had happened to my maternal grandmother.

During that same period, I also lost an uncle, then a childhood friend, with whom I'd had a strange relationship, took his own life. A boy not from my school but from my wider social milieu who at the age of fourteen, I'd coincidentally bumped into coming out of a child counsellor's office in Rathgar as I was going in. There was a kinship between us, maintained mostly over MSN Messenger. It was strange, in those days, to be a boy who was openly sad. It still is, I imagine. But there we both were. I never made a secret of it and nor did he. I don't think either of us were especially scared about what our peers would think. Both of us were always honest about who we were to those around us, and it never seemed to cost us socially.

Before he died, one of my favourite pictures of myself had been of me and him at some stupid underage disco – Touch in Rathfarnham – both of us with our fringes swept across our faces, him getting sick while lying on a plush white couch, me crouching down beside him giving a thumbs-up to the camera. What an asshole.

He killed himself when I was eighteen, after we'd been out of contact for a couple of years. The last time I ever spoke to him was over the phone at my grandfather's wake, when I'd called him to see if I could use his ID to go out drinking in town with my cousins after all the cold sandwiches had been eaten by grandaunts and granduncles we could hardly guess the names of. He'd sounded weird on the phone that day, and he couldn't help me out, and I thought nothing more of it until a couple of months later when I heard he'd died.

I went to his funeral, but I didn't go up to the casket to see him. I can't remember why I thought it was so important that I not see him lying there, dead. Foolish of me, because now I have to imagine it and, the older I get, the younger he becomes, this boy, preventably dead. People often conjure a sense of fatalism around suicide, the idea that some people are on an indivertible path to oblivion and that there is nothing to be done to save them 'from themselves'. It's not an argument I find compelling.

I know well that my proximity to death in those years was nothing special or unique. I know that people have lost closer loved ones in quicker succession and in far more dire circumstances. It just happened to be more death than I'd ever been around before. In fact, before my grandfather, virtually nobody in my life had died, save for a grandaunt or two who lived only as wraiths in my memory, dispensing Smarties and clouding my nana's living room and my five-year-old lungs with cigarette smoke and perfume that didn't smell like how perfume is supposed to smell. Between seventeen and nineteen, though, it seemed as though there was really no escaping death and its parlour tricks. There was a relentlessness to it, as though the inexorable march of time had broken into a sprint and, eventually, I turned my thoughts of death inwards.

It was around this time that I started seeing a counsellor through the college's free therapy service. I was stressed about grades, I was stressed about girls, but I was there for only one reason, which was the certainty that I was about to die.

Talking with the counsellor was a great source of comfort and I liked him a lot on a personal level, but the sessions did little to directly address my issue or, in retrospect, even understand it. At the time, I'd been under the impression that my problem was a fear of death. What a dumb way of looking at it. Who isn't afraid of death, at least on some level? Being instinctively, evolutionarily and necessarily afraid of death is the impetus at the core of almost all human behaviour. My problem was that I was afraid of death and I couldn't think about anything else.

I was unable to sleep because I was thinking about my physical body as some crude electrical appliance, wires loosely attached that could come apart at any minute and cease the momentum of the whole operation. I feared that if I slept, I would become unplugged and never wake again. But, in a sort of Rooseveltian fashion, it dawned on me before long that it wasn't death that was my problem but the fear itself. The all-consuming nature of it, the inability to look past it.

Fear to the exclusion of all else. A near-permanent physical sensation that soured all of the joys that should be resplendent in the life of a nineteen-year-old boy.

I don't believe the counsellor ever used the words 'intrusive thoughts' or suggested that there might be something truly *wrong* with me. Nothing that required a treatment plan, nothing that suggested the matter needed to be kicked up the hierarchy for some more heavy-duty looking at. Looking back, I find that strange. I was so obviously distressed, so obviously incapable of thinking about anything besides my own death and the time I was losing thinking about it. After about a year of these visits, which remained comforting but otherwise appeared to be ineffectual, the issue seemed to resolve itself. Maybe the counselling had worked after all. Maybe, at the age of twenty, I had overcome my fear of an untimely death forever.

In early 2018, I went back to my GP with my tail between my legs, ready to accept the diagnosis of OCD that had been proffered two and a half years earlier, and whatever course of action came with it. Having spent a year on a grad visa in the United States taking whatever was left of my sanity and seeing what kind of height I could drop it from like a Nokia 3210, I was finally on my last legs. I'd gone over the edge a few days before my brother's twenty-first birthday party. I'd got drunk enough to lose my phone and while I can't officially remember anything about the night, I'm almost certain I fell out of a taxi getting sick somewhere in Templeogue. If I left my phone in the car, it's probably only fair that the driver kept it as recompense.

Rudi's party itself also ended in personal disaster, when some kid fell and split his head open and, at some point, I touched a banister and soaked my arm in his blood. Lost phones, blackouts, the blood of strangers. That's the cool thing about OCD. Someone else can fall and split their head open and your first thought is, *Oh great, now I've got to deal with this stupid stranger's blood.*

What I didn't understand about OCD the first time around, when I thought I had cancer, is that it's all about intrusive thoughts.

Let me tell you about intrusive thoughts. Truly, I'd love nothing more. Maybe you already know all there is to know about them, maybe you experience them yourself. Maybe they're destroying your life too. But having encountered widespread misuse of the term online, it seems to me that it can't hurt to have another first-hand account out there in the ether.

Some intrusive thoughts are quite common. The urge to throw one's phone into a body of water or the sense, when looking over a precipice, that the abyss below is calling to you. I doubt there is anyone alive who is happy with their entire catalogue of thoughts, particularly those thoughts that come to us in a way that feels unbidden. As we established earlier, thoughts occur to us. Even the ones that feel chosen are the consequence of an ever-unfolding sequence of subatomic movements in the meat of the brain, an unseen fireworks show spelling out that which becomes our interiority.

There is a popular meme that does the rounds these days: *Bro let the intrusive thoughts win.* If you're unfamiliar with that kind of online output, the caption usually accompanies videos where someone is either behaving erratically, or in a way that may be thought of as impulsive or primal. A cat knocking a vase off a coffee table, for example. That's bro letting the intrusive thoughts win.

There is no such thing as 'letting the intrusive thoughts win' for somebody with OCD. Naturally, no two OCD-havers will be exactly alike, but that axiom appears to hold true. That's because intrusive thoughts are self-selecting; the disease actively chooses ideas that are most abominable to the host. Intrusive thoughts often revolve around themes like sickness, death, contaminating, or harming ourselves or others. They can centre on religious fears, including the unshakeable and paralysing fear that the sufferer is despised by God or destined for hell. They often include thoughts of sexual violence, particularly towards the vulnerable, thoughts that are a plague to those who suffer with them.

Intrusive thoughts are most definitely not instructional. They don't feel anything like impulses. Intrusive thoughts occur not to encourage those who have them to act a certain way, but to warn them against it. To create such an intense fear of that thing, an aversion so infernal and irrational, that the substance of the intrusive thought is all you can think about because you need to spend every moment of your life guarding against it. Every choice that you make must be made with the prevention of your fears as the top priority. You can't lift weights because you might drop one on your little dog's skull. You can't ride public transport in case you end up groping whoever sits next to you. You can't go near a live microphone in case you start blurting out some kind of racially hateful manifesto that you didn't know was buried somewhere in your mind.

People don't have intrusive thoughts because they secretly want to do all those things and are suppressing that urge – the intrusive thoughts are there because we are so horrified by the prospect of doing those things that we believe we would be better off dead. That's what happens when the intrusive thoughts win, by the way. It's not following the childlike urge to chase a pigeon through the park. It's crashing headfirst into the pavement at the foot of the seven-storey building because your mind has convinced you that you're living in a Stephen King horror story. And you can put *Bro let the intrusive thoughts win* on my headstone.

There is a cohort of people who seem to believe they understand what intrusive thoughts are, but in fact mistake them for some mythic idea of Neanderthalic impulses. Intrusive thoughts do not take the form of *I should kill the guy in front of me in the queue at the post office because he's taking too long.* In my case, for example, intrusive thoughts are a little bit more like: *Hey, remember that guy from the post office earlier? You killed him. When you got mad that he was taking so long, you sealed his fate. You're an evildoer, Carl Kinsella, and you have wrought death unto this man, who had a family to feed, by the way, you son of a bitch. But you didn't think about that, did you? You puffed out your cheeks when he wouldn't accept that his package was at a different post office and, in that moment, you killed him. And probably, by extension, his kids.*

Intrusive thoughts are, by definition, things you do not want to happen. Things you abhor. Things that make you sick to your stomach. That's why it's called 'obsessive compulsive disorder' and not 'obsessive compulsive this is how I want to feel, I love feeling this way, all of these thoughts are here by choice'. That's why they're called 'intrusive thoughts' and not 'thoughts'.

They can mess with your memory too, playing on the natural gaps that emerge in your recollection of a day. You wake up and turn on the radio to hear that a man was murdered yesterday, halfway across the country? *Well, I can't remember everything I did yesterday, so therefore …*

After enough warping under the glare of these thoughts, like a vinyl record next to a radiator, there is no reality to hold on to anymore. Nothing to keep you grounded. No reason to trust your senses or your memory, the whole Connemara wall of your existence comes crashing down and crushes you beneath the weight of everything you foolishly thought you knew about yourself and the world around you. All that's left is doubt and fear and the enduring belief that you are a monster who should be taken out behind the barn and put out of its misery.

Shortly after the 2018 doctor visit during which I gratefully accepted the diagnosis of OCD at the second time of asking, I came home from work to find that my mother had baked a cake to bring into her office the next day to share with her co-workers. Upon seeing the cake, a few thoughts occurred to me in sequence, or perhaps they occurred all at once and my conscious mind did the sequencing. It does not much matter in which order you hear them, as none of them make any damn sense.

The intrusive thoughts began to craft a narrative. They'd had a lot of practice over the previous few years. What they were telling me was this: I had in some way contaminated the cake with my blood, blood that had, all of a sudden, through the sheer willpower that seems to exist in my mind for these things, become infected with HIV.

I remember doing what I could to implement the lessons of the first few CBT sessions I'd begun attending after accepting the nature of my problem.

I thought about what I'd learned in that taupe room in Rathmines. Catch the thought. *Okay. Caught you, you son of a bitch.* Evaluate it. *Well, let's see. Did I have HIV five minutes ago?* Well, I didn't think so, but I hadn't had a test since the three I'd forked out several hundred euro for across the course of about a month at Christmas because I mistakenly used one of my parents' toothbrushes. Of course, I'd had no penetrative sex since then – it's probably self-explanatory to you that if I couldn't safely look at a cake then I wasn't exactly fucking my way across Dublin. Indeed, I have no idea why I specified it as 'penetrative sex' just now, as I was having absolutely no sex of any kind. Touching a radiator in work made me want to grab a machete and cleave off my hand at the wrist. I certainly had no desire to be inside anybody.

Continuing to evaluate the scene, I noted there was a conspicuous lack of blood, given that I had supposedly found a way to ensanguinate this cake only moments earlier.

At this point, I will pause and note that not everybody with OCD is as delusional as I was then. Indeed, most people are not, and it's even pretty rare for me these days. A year untreated in a foreign city, however, had left me holding myself together with chewing gum and toothpicks, less of a man and more of a MacGyver creation, a body and mind in utter thrall to the vagaries of a disease that had been allowed to take over root and stem. In America, I had begun to worry that coins and paper money would change, transfigure, in my hands, or magically begin to bear messages revealing my secrets to shopkeepers after I'd hand them over.

I couldn't go to restaurants there because the idea of returning a plate from whence it came became unthinkable to me. Once I noticed a wad of matchbook cardboard wedged behind the brass sconce of my apartment's front-door handle and I spent an hour working it free with a knife, just in case it bore some kind of frightening message about me (dear reader, it did not). I smashed my guitar into a thousand pieces after realising I couldn't sell it because I'd begun to have disturbing thoughts about how my DNA had poured into the wood and whether it – or indeed my thoughts – could be extracted by its new owner. I had touched it, hadn't I? My soul was seeping out into all of these things, ready to be extracted, as if someone could plug a USB cable into the crockery I'd eaten off and access the inside of my brain. How could anything be safe to leave behind? If I'd been losing my mind a year or two earlier when I thought I had cancer, then by the end of my time in New York, I had well and truly lost it.

And so it was with the cake. Before my eyes, the cake seemed to maintain a sturdy, uniform, *Great British Bake Off*-worthy presentation. It didn't look as though a madman had opened his veins and soaked the sponge in his blood. And how come there were no marks on my body, by the way? You'd think that would be compelling.

I climbed the stairs to my room and stripped naked, using my phone to video every crevice on my body, looking for a wound or a puncture mark (in case my devious plot had led me to procure a syringe while in a fugue state) or any site where my blood might have been extracted. I found none, but I didn't feel any better. All I could think about was my mother's colleagues. That tomorrow they would eat the cake that I had, with malice aforethought, poisoned with my blood.

I spent my evening as I spent most of my evenings at that time, rifling through a familiar zoetrope, a series of horrifying still images rotating around my mind. How many people would fall ill having eaten this cake, for example? Dried blood in the mouth is not how HIV is transmitted, by the way, but my brain was no longer playing by the very well-established scientific rules of our world. There was no longer any adherence to the checks and balances that keep us sane – memory, rationality, the evidence of my senses. All of that was gone. Soon I'd be carted off to Mountjoy for an utterly unprecedented and insane crime. I lay on my bed and wept.

'Why are you crying?' the doctor carrying out my colonoscopy asked, not entirely without sympathy, but clearly a bit confused. I had been crying because I'd been so sure that they were about to discover the polyps and tumours that would act as the harbingers of my doom, but even if I had not been so sure, it struck me as odd to think that a twenty-two-year-old lying sideface on a gurney getting tentacle-porned by a steel snake with a fibre-optic eye wasn't cause for at least a few tears. I watched on a screen as they explored my guts. I didn't recognise them.

It was December then. Five months had passed since I'd pulled up on my run, taken out my phone and googled whether young people could have bowel cancer. At one point, during a fit of uncharacteristic optimism, I had told my mother that if it was confirmed by colonoscopy that I didn't have cancer, I'd get a tattoo right where I thought the tumour had been to remind myself – to remind myself of I don't know what.

All I know is that when the colonoscopy results came in and I was – and you'll never believe this – cancer-free, I didn't get the tattoo. By the time the letter from the clinic had arrived to confirm that I'd wasted six months worrying, crying, starving over nothing, I had moved on to something else. I didn't feel any relief. I had got the news I wanted, of course. It's just that, by then, my mind had already mapped out the new shortest distance between wherever I was standing and total annihilation.

I was dying, or I was losing my mind.

Smoke With My Father

I WAS RAISED pretty Catholic, so I've never been able to get my head around the Mormons or any of the other more cheerful branches of Christianity. Putting on a tie and a nametag, coming to your door talking about: 'Have you heard the Good News?' *Man, what good news? Jesus was tortured to death because of us.* Being a Roman Catholic has never been about nametags, clip-on ties and practising your best salvation smile. For many of us, it's about having a statuette of a bloodied man with an invariably shredded eight-pack tacked to a cross on your wall and apologising to him as often as you can for everything you enjoy about being alive. For others, Catholicism seems to be about specifically subverting the main tenets of Jesus' teachings – you know, forgiveness, charity, selflessness, sacrifice. For very few people is it about how fun it is to be a Christian.

I'm still just enough of a Catholic that I'm not about to risk writing several paragraphs explaining why I don't believe in God. I am a gambling man, and Pascal's Wager always sounded like a smart bet to me. I will confess, though, that my doubts about God and heaven and eternity began when I was a young child. Really, God was just collateral damage in a massacre that had already succeeded in taking out the Tooth Fairy, the Easter Bunny, Tír na nÓg and Santa in short order.

Some Christmas Eve in my tween years, I walked into the living room when I should have been in bed and found my mother wrapping a games console, which I knew had been the main item of business on my brother's letter to Santa. Of course, I gave due consideration to the possibility that there was an entirely benign explanation for this activity. For example, I wondered how likely it was that perhaps Santa had brought the Xbox a day early and had tasked my mother with wrapping it. He is a busy man, of course. Ultimately, having weighed the arguments and counterarguments, I resigned myself to the realisation that the tougher kids on the school playground had been right all along, and through

Carl Kinsella

their honesty had been trying to protect me from my own naive self.

Where my belief in God came from in the first place is no mystery, at least. Both of my parents were devout Catholics throughout my childhood, at least outwardly. We went to mass every Sunday, until my Sunday league kick-off times started getting in the way. I do remember that, for a brief time, if my football team's kick-off was late enough in the day, we would actually squeeze both in, which always seemed unfair. I'm not sure how I was supposed to get into a competitive mindset while reflecting upon my sins. How are you supposed to two-foot some lad from Sheriff Street or Home Farm if you're busy wondering whether you'll be forgiven for it on a spiritual level?

My own club was Firhouse Carmel, a reference to the Carmelite order that oversaw our parish and my secondary school. Indeed, the principal of the school and several of the teachers were Carmelite priests, gliding along the cheap linoleum floors and thin carpets in their long, brown tunics. My father was the treasurer of Firhouse Carmel when I was a teenager. He attended our home games religiously (no pun intended, honestly, I'd tell you if it was) and drove me to and from every away match. For such a small club, Firhouse Carmel had a fine big pitch, eventually done away with to facilitate the construction of a Gaelscoil to accommodate this rapidly growing town on the outskirts of Dublin. For years, my father's voting patterns heavily favoured any councillor or TD who had fought against the destruction of what we called 'the main pitch'.

I had always admired the way my father, who really only learned how to work his smartphone during Covid, was able to navigate the entire county of Dublin without a GPS. It reminded me of black cab drivers in London, how they supposedly know every street in the city. Somehow my father knew every pitch, every park, every close, every grove, every football club in Dublin. Sometimes, some of my teammates would miss kick-off because their mam or dad had taken a wrong turn. In all those years of being driven around by my father, it only happened to me once.

When mass and football began to overlap, my father instigated a policy of 'leaving after Communion', which is exactly what it sounds like. Brazening out the first and second reading, getting through the sign of peace, wolfing down the Communion, bending a knee to the Lord and then getting out of dodge until next week. Most weeks, I would actually turn to my father during mass and ask him outright if we could leave after Communion, a request I'm quite sure he never denied.

In the car itself, I had a very clear ritual that my father never saw fit to interrupt. Depending on what age I was, I'd plug in the earphones of my Tesco-brand discman or my Creative Zen or my iPod shuffle and I'd blare either of My Chemical Romance's first two albums, singing along at a volume that could only be described as 'neurodivergent', while my father politely ignored me and listened – tried to listen – to the radio. You know he never once asked me to stop? Now, granted, he is entirely deaf in one ear and mostly deaf in the other, but surely all the more reason to tell your son – this weird little Steven Gerrard/Gerard Way hybrid you've produced – to sack it off with the singing for even one journey. He never asked that of me.

My father had great belief in my footballing abilities, though, in the grand scheme of things, I was really no better than decent. I had a knack for making the right choices on the pitch and, for a couple of years, it seemed I was faster than just about every defender I came up against, but my technical ability was always lacking. I have a tendency to panic on the ball when I don't have enough time to think, and in front of goal when I have too much time to think. One Sunday morning, during a particularly dry spell in front of goal, I wrapped a brown cloth Carmelite scapular around my wrist. I scored that day, so I wore the scapular the next couple of weeks and kept scoring. Eventually, God must have figured out he wasn't getting anything out of the deal and the goals dried up.

A combination of fallen arches, shin splints, lower back pain, an inability to acclimatise to new groups of men, and an utter refusal to train twice a week has kept me from playing any kind of organised football for the last six or seven years, and maybe I'm beginning to understand what a miracle it is to have a ball at your feet, the exaltation of skinning your marker, the divination of choosing the exact right finish and watching the ball hit the net.

But as a younger man, I never understood the professional athletes who would so effusively thank God after a big win, the whole 'glory to God' business. This might be a Catholic thing too. The God I grew up with didn't ask us to accumulate glory on earth and pass it up to him. I remember being explicitly told to reflect upon all the ways in which I was unglorious. Jesus was actually painfully clear about the amassing of material glory on earth, so what would he think about trophies, gold medals and lucrative sponsorship deals?

Of course, the Vatican is so rich that nobody even knows how rich it is, but this appears to be an exception of some kind that Jesus probably included off the books. Luke 6:20– 21 reads: 'Looking at his disciples, he said: "Blessed are you who are poor, for yours is the kingdom of God. Blessed are you who hunger now, for you will be satisfied. Blessed are you who weep now, for you will laugh."' Maybe he then said, under his breath: 'But if you'd like to build an opulent city-state that eventually regains its sovereignty through a back-alley deal with the father of modern fascism, that is also fine.' Maybe if I were as rich as a Premier League football player or a pope, I'd have a better understanding of why they feel the need to point to the sky after scoring a goal. The footballers, I mean, though the pope may do something similar if he feels he's given an especially good homily. Maybe not the new guy, but the last guy was Argentinian, so he probably got it. To me, though, it would make more sense for a Catholic footballer to celebrate a goal by rending his garments or washing his opponent's feet with his hair. Would not that be a truer tribute to our Lord? By eighteen, I was a lapsed Catholic and more or less a lapsed soccer player.

When justifying their falling from grace with God, many lapsed Catholics will tell you that they have a lot of admiration for Jesus. Sort of like how you might not be able to stomach Man United but, to make peace with your uncle who supports them, you can talk about how you've always respected Roy Keane. To this day, we know very little for certain about Jesus' life and the historicity thereof. It appears to be the scholarly consensus that there was a man named Jesus who lived and died in that part of the world at that time. While the synoptic gospels of Matthew, Mark and Luke differ significantly in parts from the gospel of John ('Lamb of God' as one of Jesus' titles only appears in the non-synoptic gospel, for example), there are a few points of agreement, specifically around the cleansing of the temple. That was the episode in which Jesus caught a bunch of merchants and moneylenders operating out of the Second Temple in Jerusalem, completely lost the rag, and started flipping tables like he'd just lost on *Come Dine With Me*. It is more or less the case that all we really know for sure about Jesus is that he was born, he died and, somewhere in between, he went totally nuts at least once. We also know that Christ was not his last name, but more of a title. He was not Christ-comma-Jesus, but rather Jesus *the* Christ. Sort of like Megan *thee* Stallion, or Kermit *the* Frog.

The Last Supper, the final gathering of all Jesus' apostles before his crucifixion, is a scene I think about often. Imagine showing up to a party your friend is throwing only for him to insist upon washing your feet, making all thirteen of you sit on one side of a long table while he mysteriously prophesies that one of you will betray him and claims that the meal has been made of his own flesh and blood. Of course, anyone who's ever seen a friend take their recreational cocaine usage too far will have experienced this or something similar, but that's not the image Jesus otherwise cultivated. Although he did also take up preaching around the age of thirty-one, telling people he was the Son of God Almighty and that anyone who pleased him would be seated at his side in the Kingdom of Heaven, and all that. I'm just saying, if one of my friends started pulling that shit now out of nowhere, I know what powdery white substance I'd instinctively blame.

I have this theory — not one of my more well-grounded theories — that if you ever really believed in God, then it's impossible to stop. You can live your life as though you believe he doesn't exist, in much the same way we walk the earth as though it is still, rather than hurtling through space and turning on its axis, but some habits can't be unlearned. Don't you think in prayers? Isn't there some semi-silent subcurrent to your being that pulls and pushes, a gravity that hangs like a hand, reaching out into everything that isn't there just in case something is?

Both of my parents stopped going to mass between 2010 and 2012, a period during which three of my grandparents died. My other grandfather, Charlie, the man for whom I am named, had died when my father was about twenty-seven, around the time he left home and moved to Dublin. Raised in abject poverty on the side of a road outside Wexford town, as a young child my father had no access to running water, and he, his six siblings and four half-siblings chopped wood for warmth and cut the heads off chickens for food. At some point or another, he left school and his childhood ended.

My father does not have stories about university, about debating societies or trips abroad with his friends. My father has stories about working on a farm and being caught in the rain, sneaking into a barn and wrapping himself in the first fluffy stuff he could find only to realise he'd snuggled himself up in fibreglass and cut himself to ribbons. I don't know how he knows all of the stuff he knows. Sometimes, when I think about how much time the previous generation had for reading, my insides go cold. Then I remember I've never had to wrap myself in fibreglass or cut the head off a chicken. It doesn't make me any more grateful for my own privileges but it really lets me off the hook about not reading more.

When I was young, very young, like before I could read, my father used to quiz me on the world capitals. I don't think I had any idea what a 'capital' was – indeed, at that age I had only been introduced to the concept of 'England' through two different *Muppets* VHS tapes – but I thoroughly enjoyed how impressed my father seemed to be that I could remember things. My favourite was Morocco, whose capital is Rabat. This was almost certainly because it sounded a bit like Batman who, as far as I knew, was just the guy from my pyjamas.

My father's mother died shortly before he turned sixty, the same summer my maternal grandmother did. Between the pain of the loss and the mounting evidence of the Church's many sick abuses throughout the history of modern Ireland, I don't think my parents could justify to themselves going to mass anymore. There are undoubtedly many such cases. The collapse in mass attendance across Ireland has been well documented. Still, I'd like to survey my fellow lapsed Catholics someday and ask them if they can tell me, without equivocation, that they no longer believe in God. That they do not feel pangs of judgement, or appeal to some greater unseen mercy as a matter of course. By the time of the Great Grandparent Rapture, God had certainly been relegated in my mind – more of a superstition than an all-knowing, all-powerful, all-loving Creator, little more than a scapular wrapped round a wrist – but it was uncomfortable to watch both my parents lose not just their own parents, but the pillars of faith that I'd assumed would be a permanent fixture of their lives.

I didn't even really realise that I'd been raised Catholic until I was in my twenties, when I started to meet people who weren't brought to mass as children, who had never been Confirmed and therefore only had three names as opposed to my more pious four, whose grandmothers had not felt compelled to add the words 'please God' to the end of any statement that made use of the future tense. I'd had quite a simplistic and monolithic idea of what it meant to be raised in Ireland, and that rearing included Sunday mornings spent kneeling, then standing, then kneeling, then sitting, then standing again, and occasionally blessing yourself, all while using the forty-five minutes to luxuriate in thoughts about the various sins that you were nominally there to purge. Some of my most detailed sexual-fantasy scenarios were painstakingly constructed in the time that mass provided, and I suspect the same is true for Catholics the world over.

In my first year of secondary school, I went to mass in the prayer room every Wednesday morning of Lent. I don't think I knew at the time why I was doing it, and I don't think I've worked it out since, but it does fit several patterns of behaviour that have endured throughout my life.

The first is a tendency to exaggerate my own Catholicism. Not the extent to which I am a believer in the teachings of the Catholic dogma, of course, but perhaps the extent to which Catholicism was a decisive cultural influence in my life. There are elements of my personality that I blame on the

Church that could just as easily be blamed on mental illness, for example, or just by being sort of a shitty person.

The second is a desperate need for attention, usually achieved by obnoxiously subverting the expectations that I believe other people might have of me. Mercifully, for all involved, I've managed to tone this down over the years (he says, while writing a book). As a teenager, though, it was pretty insufferable. I would turn up to football training in a Slipknot T-shirt instead of a football jersey just to prove a point, that I was still good at football even if I liked Slipknot. The only catch was that I didn't really like Slipknot all that much. I could only ever name, like, four Slipknot songs. And yeah, they're fine, but I didn't need the T-shirt. I had an Iron Maiden poster on my bedroom wall for years. I couldn't even identify an Iron Maiden song if it came on the radio. Not now, not then. I listened to 50 Cent, Eminem, Nas, Jay-Z, Beyoncé and a whole rake of chart-topping acts more than I listened to the bands whose stickers were on my guitar.

Before returning to school for my third year, when I was fourteen years old, I dyed my naturally strawberry-blond hair jet black – a Tom DeLonge mop atop a pallid, freckled face that made for an unholy sight. I bought a girls' schoolbag and pencil case and, on top of this motley assortment of awful accoutrements, I purchased a pair of dock shoes, like the ones the rich kids from my year wore. I know you're supposed to be kind to your younger self but, Jesus Christ, you've got to draw a line somewhere. In retrospect, I can identify that I did these things because I wanted to know – no, I wanted to prove – that people would still like me even if I did things that were outside of the social norm. They did, in what is either a rare testament to the mercy of young men or an equally rare testament to just how great a guy I am to be around.

The first friend I ever consciously made was a boy in my first-year class named Paul. He had red hair, real red hair, mismatched with his dark brown eyes and a tan. He was beautiful, and seemingly beloved by everyone who'd attended the junior school with him. The two of us had volunteered to play music at the first-year mass, which meant we got to hang out in the chapel that sat on the school grounds, nestled between the lake and the rugby pitches. I was barely good enough to pull off 'Wake Me Up When September Ends' by Green Day but I managed. The other song we played was 'Where Is My Mind?', a song by The Pixies that Paul had played for me days before. The first time I heard that three-note riff, I could have kissed him on the mouth. For whatever reason, Paul decided he wanted to keep me as a friend, and from that point on, pretty much everyone else in our year was my friend too.

You have to understand that this was a generation of boys who had been raised on *School of Rock*, and that this was a period in history when playing a guitar solo in a church during a school mass was regarded as kind of a cool thing to do. It no longer feels like the kind of thing that kids would find cool.

Perhaps the most pathetic thing about me, as a man in my thirties, and there is stiff competition by the way, is that I am desperate for you to know that I was well-liked in secondary school. For some reason, I seem to think that this is like … a five-star review of my character. I seem to believe, implicitly, that having once won the approval of roughly a hundred thirteen-year-old boys is one of the most clear-cut affirmations of my worth as a human being. *Oh, you think I'm a loser, do you? Well, call up some of the kids from my secondary school and ask them how much I made them laugh in honours English, why don't you? Then we'll see who's a loser.*

That's not to say that I found secondary school easy. At the time, I'd probably have told you that I hated just about every minute. I hated that I had priests for teachers. I hated that I wasn't allowed to talk whenever I wanted, not allowed to drink from my water bottle or go to the bathroom without permission. Not allowed to spend all day showing off how smart I was. Something about being in school did something to my perception of time, consigning me to my own version of Zeno's paradox. Sure, maybe the first class of the day would be over by 9.30 a.m., but in order to reach 9.30 a.m. we first had to reach 8.46 a.m. In order to reach 8.46 a.m. we first had to reach 8.45 and 999 milliseconds a.m., and so on.

Sitting on those decades-old chairs, my shaky-leg syndrome so bad it lifted my plywood desk off the floor, I could never see to the end. I could never make my body understand that this was only a temporary state of affairs. Sitting still felt as though I had a lump of coal smouldering at the bottom of my stomach, and I would shift endlessly in my seat, look endlessly out the window and write truly awful poetry in the margins of my copybooks.

The traditional teaching method – a grown-up standing at the top of the classroom, reading unenthusiastically and occasionally with arbitrary and vindictive rage from a textbook – has never worked on me. I've only ever been able to learn one way, which is by reading on my own time. Much of my time in school was spent reading the textbook and ignoring whatever was happening in the classroom, and my grades didn't suffer. It's precisely because my grades didn't suffer that all of the other stuff went unaddressed, and I suspect that, these days, a child with a similar personality profile would be quite quickly medicated. God knows I'm medicated now but, back then, I was a skilled practitioner in the art of what young people call 'rawdogging reality'.

In second year, the year head – who was a priest – became obsessed with making sure that my hair was above my eyebrows in the front and above my collar at the back. On a regular basis, he would do the rounds of our classrooms and say my name in that low, sonorous tone so many priests seem to share – voices perfect for maintaining the illusion of comfort even as they speak of apocalyptic revelations and the mind-bending prospect of eternity. He would say my name and make a snip-snip motion with his fingers. One day, he told me that if I didn't get my hair cut that evening, I shouldn't come into school the next day. I told my mother this and, perhaps in an early offering of evidence that she may not have been as devout a Catholic as I'd imagined, she sided with me. I didn't go to school the next day, and the day after that she took me to a ladies' salon and sent me into school halfway through the day as if to make the point that, yes, I had been intentionally kept out of school on account of the demands that had been made of my hair. The haircut I got made me look like Julie Andrews, but I'm over that now.

There are at least 166 days in the Irish school year, times that by three for the years I spent in that school before I more or less gave up on secondary education and – seeking to abbreviate the senior cycle – begged my parents to move me to a school in the city centre that had girls, no uniforms, no religious influence and no transition year, meaning I'd be out of school just two months after turning seventeen. By my sixth year, the school I'd moved to made no effort to keep tabs on whether students turned up to class or not, relying only on sign-in sheets. I had effectively dropped out of school by then, spending my days in coffee shops around town, writing songs, texting my girlfriend and nursing the anxiety bubbling in my stomach over whether I'd ever be caught. To alleviate my own guilt at mitching, I would often go to St Teresa's church, the one down the laneway on the left side of Grafton Street, and pray for forgiveness for not being in school. If I am still a Catholic then that's the kind of Catholic I am. Ashamed and in permanent pursuit of forgiveness, from anyone, for anything.

But I digress. 166 x 3 is 498. Assuming a school day is eight hours total, including an hour for lunch, that's 3,984 hours spent with that same group of boys, all while we were our rawest selves, unrehearsed and undiluted and unable to conceal what we were. We would torture teachers, ordinary working people, many of whom were probably even younger than I am now. People whom I can imagine sympathising with over a drink. *Those kids did what?* One time a yearmate of mine threw a chair through a second-storey window for no immediately apparent reason, and I remember my friend Conall rolling his eyes and asking, 'Do you think they have to put up with this shit in Blackrock?' Bins got set on fire, breast pockets got torn off, bags got emptied, turned inside out and then refilled and zipped up. Cocks were Tipp-Exed onto every available unguarded surface. One time, when we were in a fight, Paul did my schoolbag so bad that I had to buy a new one.

We were so undistracted then, unencumbered by the outside world, by the unrelenting access to narratives about ourselves that swarm around today's children. We had to make our own fun, we had to sneak behind the hedges in the yard to pass around one can of cider as if that made a goddamn lick of sense, we had to kick doors off their hinges and melt our pens with Bunsen burners and set each other's hair on fire. We had to find a way to fill all of that time, working together to find ways to waste our youth. That much was entirely intuitive.

Fights, known to us as 'straighteners', would be scheduled at the lakelands area of the school grounds to settle disputes over girls or personality clashes or sometimes just for gladiatorial entertainment. I avoided the violence for the most part – who would ever want to hurt little old me, after all? – though I did once land a punch I was very proud of right into the ribs of my good friend Rob. He was about 6 foot 4 and played on the rugby team, and I was delighted with myself until he picked me up and dump-tackled me on the hard, flat surface of my school desk. It should tell you how tiny I was that I didn't break clean through the thing like in a WWE Tables, Ladders and Chairs match. I was so winded, I thought I was dying, or that my spine had broken, and when I opened my mouth to speak I found that I could not. I had the sense to wait it out – sense might not be the right word, as waiting it out wouldn't have been the perfect move if I'd really been dying – and about twenty minutes into the next class my breathing returned to normal.

Rob and I hadn't been fighting for any reason in particular; it's just that when teenage boys spend a minimum of 3,984 hours in each other's company, occasionally they'll try to put each other through a table. In fact, it's a miracle that it only happened once. We're still good friends, Rob and I. I was at the second day of his wedding. I suspect I'd have been invited to the wedding proper had I not left the school after third year – had I made any effort whatsoever to stay in his life, this boy whom I claim to love dearly.

The night of our debs – which I was allowed to attend despite having left the school – we were on a party bus out to some nightclub in Naas. I'd spent the first few hours of the evening in the school's main hall, necking wine nervously and making sure everyone who hadn't seen me for the previous couple of years knew I had a hot girlfriend. Everyone was already well-past-gone by the time we were on that party bus, climbing over the seats, pissing into beer bottles, risking broken necks if the bus were to stop short. At some point during the journey, Rob pulled me close. We were two eighteen-year-old-boys and he held my face against his neck and told me, 'You know who your friends are, you know who loves you', and I spent the next few years hoping he meant it forever because God knows once the night was over and they'd given us our chicken fillet rolls and put us on a bus back to Dublin, I didn't text him or see him again for another three years.

Another one of the boys I'd spent that night with died suddenly, in his sleep, shortly after I turned twenty-six. Just about everyone I'd been friends with at school went to the funeral at the humanist chapel in Mount Jerome. I remember so much about him. A painful, embarrassing amount. The orange Timberland hoodie he wore to school most days, how his hair looked when it was cut short against his scalp, his golden curls when he let it grow long. I remember the time in first year when he'd chipped his tooth, how cool it made him look, how my mother would have killed me if I'd ever come home with that same broken, rakish smile. I remember the first time he ever messaged me on MSN Messenger, and how it felt like I'd been canonised. I remember a time I had ditched class to hide in a bathroom stall, hearing his voice out by the sinks talking to another boy from my year – one who would end up in jail, at least briefly – and I remember their horror as I allowed the cubicle door to creep slowly open, letting them think they'd been caught on the hop by a teacher, only to step forward out of the shadows. I remember how hard we laughed, how good it felt to be with them in that moment.

I remember sitting with around six other boys on his single bed getting ready to walk to some stupid underage disco, and I remember being the one to carry the cans in my backpack because I wanted to make myself useful. He's been dead for six years, but I remember him very well. I remember him better than I ever actually knew him to begin with, I think. Miss him more than I ever bothered to love him. Mourn him more than I ever bothered to be his friend while he was alive.

Someone once told me that if you remember something in great detail, then that means it must have made you very happy. I'm sure there are exceptions, but I more or less agree. It has always seemed to me that there is never anything to remember from the worst times. The times spent with your whole body under the covers until you finally give in to make a cup of tea, watching the water bring the bag to the bottom of the mug as the steam rises and the gold billows and spreads and you pray it will be enough to stave off the dread for long enough to keep you alive. The times spent rewatching your favourite boxset or Netflix series, rereading your favourite books because anything new would simply be too disruptive to your heart beating like butterfly wings against a shut window. The times spent suppressing your very existence, wishing your soul would recede to your innermost, cavernous core lest it be further damaged by whatever misery your physical body is enduring in that moment. These moments give us little to look back on. They are the same moment, a record that skips on a bum note, like sitting on the back seat of the family car trying to read a book after dark. Catching the same word over and over with each passing streetlight. Persevering even though you know you'll never get anywhere.

There are people I have lost through my own carelessness. There are people I have lost on purpose. There are people I've lost even though I did everything I could think of to get them to stay. But there are some people I just lost. Nothing to do with me, they're just gone. There are things I'd been meaning to ask them, conversations I was so sure I would have with them some day. If I could live that moment again, the first thing I'd do is tell you I love you. If I could live that moment a thousand times, I might eventually learn something.

In the lead-up to his retirement, my father started to go to mass again. My parents live directly across the road from our local church, and their home is separated from the priests' house by about half a football pitch of green space, and a single wall that my brother and I used as a goal for heads and volleys and World Cup when we were children. My mother speculated that my father's decision to return to the flock was mostly a social venture. As part of his role as treasurer of our local football club, he's spent just about every Friday night for the past twenty years going to the local pub to 'sell raffle tickets' for the club's monthly draw. There is no doubt that he sells the tickets, but I suspect had there been no tickets to sell, he might just have found his way to the pub anyway. My mother saw the short walk to mass of a Sunday morning as an extension of this ritual. Round two, as it were.

This made sense to me. If Firhouse had a mayor, it's plausible that my father would run for the office, and I suspect that the two pillars of his campaign would be his appearances at mass and his appearances at the pub, especially now that he brings the dog (to the pub, not to mass, yet). My younger brother disagrees with that reading of my father, though. He has a much more earnest take – that my father, now in his seventies, was trying to get right with God. I think it's probably a bit of both.

Besides, the older you get, the less you need any excuse to do anything at all. I'm no fan of work, don't get me wrong, but watching a man retire at sixty-five in this day and age is a little strange. Sixty-five is not young by any stretch, but my father had spent his life doing two things: working, and driving my brother and me to soccer matches. The chauffeur role was one my father seemed to approach with total acceptance, like a 'One must imagine Sisyphus happy' kind of thing.

And my father's chauffeuring wasn't limited to football. In late 2017, An Garda Síochána reopened its investigation into the Kerry babies case. On 14 April 1984, a baby's body washed up on Kerry's White Strand. He was found five days after he was born, and two days after he died. He had been stabbed no fewer than twenty-eight times. I wanted to cover the reopening story for the publication I was working for at the time, and my dad offered to drive me down to Kerry so I could sit in a garda station press room with crime correspondents and high-profile TV presenters like Miriam O'Callaghan and go through the town asking locals what they thought of the whole thing. It was at least a five-hour drive each way, and rather than spend the journey talking, I did what I'd been doing my whole life – since he'd first started driving me to football matches – I put my earphones in and I tuned the world out.

As I alluded to earlier, my father has been mostly deaf since childhood. A mysterious condition that, the way he tells it, seems to have been either caused or desperately exacerbated by medical malpractice. Oh, to be a child in early 1960s Ireland. He never learned sign language, and doesn't wear a hearing aid – though I'm not sure the latter would even help in his case. He moves through the world as though he is not deaf, which is certainly an interesting choice for somebody who … is. A psychoanalyst once told me that by doing nothing to mitigate his deafness, my father was choosing not to hear me. Definitely score one for the people who adopt the Homer Simpson attitude that shrinks exist primarily to tear families apart. I didn't really buy what my therapist had to say, even if it was a little cathartic to hear.

It's tempting to blame my father for all of the things I don't like about myself and my way of being. I think it is much to his credit that if there is any one person in my life who could bear the brunt of being blamed for all of my problems and keep moving forward, keep loving me, it's probably him. But what would it say about me? The boy – and let's be honest, 'boy' is a generous descriptor for someone on the cusp of turning twenty-five – who, while in receipt of such an enormous favour, would deafen himself to ten hours that could have been spent speaking with the man who has most earned his time.

I have never felt that my father doesn't listen to me. He doesn't know how to ask me about my problems, sure, but that's a pretty high bar to set for someone whose historical figureheads for mental illness are probably Charles Manson and the guy from *The Shining*.

Sometimes, I'll sit around and think about things I should text my father.

Hey Dad, did you watch the match?

Hey Dad, do you know what is the only capital outside of the USA named for a United States president?

Hey Dad, did you ever read Heart of Darkness?

Hey Dad, what do you think will happen to me after you're gone?

I never send them.

There is an unease of sorts to my relationship with my father, though I'm not sure he feels it, or knows it. If he does, then I get the sense he's not too worried about it, which is actually a great comfort. This presumably is a very unexceptional state of affairs between a father and son, at least if that song about the cat and the cradle is to be believed.

He is a singular man. He has few hobbies besides watching horse-racing on TV, even the ones he hasn't bet on. He didn't grow up with horses, he just likes watching them run. He loves to watch cricket, even though he was brought up in the least 'cricket' circumstances I can imagine.

Once, when I was coming home from town, he texted me to see if I wanted to watch the Liverpool match in our local. It was Salah's first season at Liverpool and he scored the opening goal in a 1–1 draw with Chelsea, which means the date was 25 November 2017. It was one of the rare occasions when I took my chance and tried bluntly to figure my father out. I asked him how he stays so zen about everything and he told me that he takes life one day at a time. I asked him if he was aware that some people, such as his son sitting before him, spend their entire lives in therapy trying to achieve a similar state of being. 'I suppose they do,' he replied. That's about as far as I got.

My father loves to smoke. I remember him sitting on the concrete step outside our back door when I was a child, smoking a cigarette in the evening. As a panicky child, it would have taken me no time at all to raise the matter with him when I first learned from a TV ad or a cigarette carton that 'Smoking Kills'. I don't remember what exactly put it in my head, but when I was five or six, I begged him to stop smoking, lest he consign himself to a quick and painful death, and he told me he would stop, and it really meant a lot to me. As much as something can really mean to a five-year-old child who, at that point, is probably still struggling with concepts like 'tomorrow' and 'how good it feels to abuse substances'. I trusted that he was telling the truth, which he wasn't, because who on earth would stop smoking because some dumbass five-year-old who can barely do all the capitals of Europe asked them to?

As you might expect from this perennially unworried creature, my father never went to too much trouble to hide his enduring habit. He put together enough of a masquerade to fool a five-year-old for a couple of years, and that was about it. Box-shaped indentations in the breast pocket of his suit jacket near the golden pin he'd received for donating blood, the red-and-white branding visible in backpacks and suitcases when we would pack for holidays.

One time, my mother and I surprised him in the local pub, and we walked in on him tipping a cigarette into an ashtray. This was before the smoking ban, so I was still pretty young.

Once again, I begged my father to quit and, once again, he told me he would and, once again, I believed him and, once again, he didn't.

He continued to smoke in secret, and it didn't really come up again until I was fourteen and we were on a football trip to Munich. I was captain of the team by then, having been aided in no small part by my father's advice to shoot low and hard, always pass the ball if there was someone in a better position, never go across your own goal, and when you've beaten your man, don't go back to beat him again. We'd been staying in a hotel and on one of the evenings I came downstairs to find my father smoking once more, but I didn't say anything to him this time. Feeling betrayed, I went back up to my room and cried.

To this day, I appreciate my roommate for not making a big deal out of it. We were fourteen-year-old boys on a football team, after all. He could have buried me then and there, but he didn't. He was sympathetic to my sensitivity, but he, like most of the kids I had ever raised the matter with, didn't care if or whether his parents smoked. Or, at least, he didn't see it as something that should define the way he saw his parents.

I, unknowingly, was the abnormal one for spending my childhood wrapped up in resentment simply because my father indulged in this one simple vice amongst all of the favours, all of the dedication, the setting of an entire life to one side to make sure I had everything I could ever have needed. But I didn't want to lose him, and I thought I would, and I never knew what to do about it. Maybe if, instead of telling me he'd quit, he'd told me that life was long and hard, and that he had already given up so much for me, maybe I'd have understood then. Instead, he tried to contort himself for my benefit, and all I ever did was punish him for it.

Teenager or not, how was it possible for me to be so unsympathetic? I understood what it meant to be a man. I'd heard Johnny Cash's version of 'Hurt'. Hearing 'Hurt', understanding its context and, ideally, seeing the music video, is a formative moment in any young man's life. The moment we realise, *Oh, so that's how it's going to feel when I'm an old, old man and I realise I've totally blown it? What was that he said? 'Empire of dirt', was it?* Somehow, this was not enough to spare my father my judgement. I thought his behaviour was unnatural and unreasonable, and it took me too long to realise that the opposite had been true all along. I don't necessarily think I'm a bad son, but I am myopic about my own concerns – such as whether or not my father is a smoker – to the point of corrupting my own experience of life. There is no question that this attitude makes me a worse person, and not a better one. I long to be the birthday card version of myself: 'To a brilliant son', 'To the best big brother'. Come on, guys, who do we think we're fooling here?

Recently, I got a phone call from my mother to tell me that my dad had fallen in the middle of the night in the back garden and split his head open. He'd got up to let the dog out without turning on any lights or putting on his glasses, just shambling about in too-long pyjama legs until he eventually fell, the back of his head taking the brunt. My mother told me she realised something was wrong when Arya came back upstairs alone, and so she went to check on my father. She got no response when she called his name, and through the aperture of the back door, she could only see his slippered feet pointed towards the sky. There is only one thing she could have been thinking in that moment, though I'm not sure she truly had time to process the scene before my father spoke up softly and confirmed that he was alive, and that he'd fallen over his pyjama bottoms. My mother asked him had he hit his head and he told her no, only for her to lift him and find the back of his hair slick with fresh blood. He declined an ambulance, of course, agreeing to visit the VHI clinic the next morning. He had already reneged on that deal by the time she called me.

When she told me that he'd refused to get his head checked out the next morning, I was ready to snap. Though she agreed with me, she told me that she'd kept him awake all night and done whatever it is you're supposed to do if you're worried somebody might have a concussion. She'd asked him what year it was, what day it was tomorrow, what he was supposed to be doing. She'd asked him birthdays – mine and my brother's – which, honestly, I would have been surprised for him to get on the first try even if he hadn't suffered head trauma. Apparently, he'd done well on my mother's ad hoc concussion quiz and so he was let off the hook. I called him, ready to let him have it over his recklessness, but I just couldn't bring myself to get angry again. What a waste of time. Instead, I said something like: 'You know, you really should have gotten it checked out?' and he accepted that he should have and that's where we left it. I let him know that Mam had told me she'd been quizzing him all sorts of things and he confirmed she had.

'What's the capital of Morocco?' I asked him, and he got it right.

'I'll never forget that one,' he said.

In the end, it is my father's approach to his life and his health that has been vindicated, not mine. Even his decision not to get himself checked out after his fall is entirely in line with whatever philosophy he has cultivated. There'd been another time in my late teens when he came home from a work Christmas party and fell up the stairs while carrying a cup of tea. I slept through it somehow, but whatever way he fell, the tea ended up on the ceiling and he ended up breaking his collarbone badly enough that it still protrudes uncomfortably upwards as if it's about to burst out of his skin. He was told at the time that they could correct it with surgery, which he decided against, because that's the kind of guy he is. He doesn't care if he can hear, he doesn't care if his collarbone looks normal. He has his way of life, and I have mine. Smoking may not be the wisest course of action, but it's better than spending your life caring about things you can't control, getting angry at the people you love because you've decided that loving them so much gives you the right. The thing about trying to squeeze blood from a stone is that if you stick with it long enough, you will get blood eventually. It's just that it'll be yours. Your time would be better spent sitting in your back garden, smoking with someone who forgave you something, someone you forgave.

These bodies were not made to comfort themselves. The heart was not made to silence its own rabbiting beat. I think that while we're living, most of us are lucky enough to find at least one person — a parent, a sibling, a lover, a friend — with whom we want nothing more than to share everything. To see our lives illuminated through their eyes, these people who take our otherwise disordered time on this earth and turn it into something that seems celestially ordained, which it is.

I don't have a coherent idea of an afterlife, but it does bring me some comfort to imagine a sort of simple ante-dimension between this life and whatever comes next. Little more than a small campfire in a redwood grove on a warm night, thousands of feet above sea level, as close to the sky as can be, the planets spinning an unnatural aurora overhead. A chance to meet once again with those people who made life something worth embracing. It may not have made me feel alive to live it, but it makes me feel alive to tell it to you now. It would take an entire afterlife, after all, to explain every impulse behind every thought behind every action behind every moment. To wring every drop from this life, this life that is little more than a collection of things we reclaim from a void. Shells and bottle caps and dug-up old coins spread out across a picnic blanket laid on the soft, white sand.

The day ends and the sun sets more suddenly than you thought it would, and the indigo of the sky stretches imperishably ahead. In the light we're losing, we survey what we have salvaged. The families we were born into or the ones we made. The people we loved and the people we lost. The smooth curves and the sharp, gleaming edges of every moment we held in our hearts, throbbing and trembling like a fist clenched around a knife. Souvenirs of love and pain, sorrow, regret, joy, anticipation, the connective tissue of our existence from moment to moment. Every sensation that washed over our grateful consciousness, before being called home, like the tides by the moon.

Acknowledgements

I have always wanted to know what it would be like to prove my doubters wrong but, unfortunately, most of the people I've encountered in my life have been unfailingly supportive, patient and prepared to back me in my ambitions.

First and foremost, I want to give my heartfelt thanks to my editor, Joanna Smyth, for all her work in making this book what it is and bearing with me and my dubious relationship with deadlines. I would like to express my deepest gratitude also to Ciara Doorley and the wider team at Hachette Ireland for being so helpful from the very first moment and giving me the opportunity to share these essays with the world. This gratitude absolutely extends to the freelancers who worked on this book, including my copy-editor Aonghus Meaney and my cover designer Emma Rogers.

There are many editors and mentors whose generous wisdom and guidance I've benefited from over the years, including but not limited to Sinéad O'Carroll, Susan Daly, Daragh Brophy, Christine Bohan, Paddy McKenna, Dion Fanning and Conor Heneghan. Thank you all for making me better at what I do. At the outset of this project, I received invaluable advice from Aoife Barry, Patrick Freyne, Conor Nagle, Nicky Ryan, Amy Clarkin and Rosanna Cooney, and I am very fortunate to have had their time and consideration.

I wrote this book while working full-time, and I'd like to thank the entire team at Journal Media Ltd for their understanding as I undoubtedly messed up parts of my actual job in the service of what was, essentially, just a fun thing that I wanted to do. Similarly, I would like to thank Louise McSharry for her kind support, both professionally and personally, over the past two years.

I'm beyond blessed to have so many friends who make this life so worth living and worth writing about. It feels utterly absurd to me to narrow down the seemingly endless list of people whom I am so lucky to know. To Lily, Mike, Cormac, Jamie, Kit, Emily, Whooley, Tom, Johnny, Megan, Matthew and literally dozens more, I will never be able to thank you enough. In time, I hope to publish a several-hundred-page, Tolkien-esque appendix to this book, which includes everyone I'd like to thank and exactly why.

To my mother, Maura, I can scarcely think of what to say. I would be nowhere without you, and there is no two ways about it. I owe you everything. To my father, Michael, I hope that being thanked in the acknowledgements of a book supplants skydiving in the late 1980s as your go-to story to tell when you want to sound cool. I love you both more than anything, and I hope I've made you proud. To Rudi, my best friend, you make me proud every day, and watching you thrive is one of my very favourite things about being alive. To Rachel, it has been so wonderful getting to know you, and I hope you know that you are a part of our family. And to Arya. You are a dog, and not an especially bright dog, but I hope on some level you can perceive how much joy you've brought into our lives. As I write this passage, I can already imagine the blankness of your little face when my mother inevitably reads it to you.

To my family at large, my aunts, uncles, cousins … It's just downright improbable that I should get to spend my life among such caring, loving, wonderful people. I am in no doubt that we can all agree this state of affairs is thanks in no small part to the influence of my late nana and granddad, May and William Connell, whom I miss terribly. To my family in Wexford and Carlow, I know that we don't speak as often as we should, but you are always in my heart – in particular, my godfather Billie Kinsella, who died during the writing of this book. *Ar dheis Dé go raibh a anam.*

Lastly, I'd like to thank you, and indeed anyone who has ever read my writing – whether it amused you, bored you, thrilled you or moved you to such a rage that you felt the need to email me. I try not to take this privilege for granted, and while I don't always live up to that goal, I remain keenly aware that I am stupidly lucky in this respect, among so many others.